THE
IMITATION
OF
CHRIST

THE ESSENTIAL WISDOM LIBRARY

Buddhism

The Tao Te Ching

The Bhagavad Gita

St. Francis of Assisi

The Kebra Nagast

The Toltec Way

The Kybalion

Orthodoxy

The Dhammapada

THE
IMITATION
OF
CHRIST

THE COMPLETE ORIGINAL EDITION

THE ESSENTIAL WISDOM LIBRARY

THOMAS À KEMPIS

TRANSLATED BY JOHN PAYNE
INTRODUCTION BY JON M. SWEENEY

ST. MARTIN'S
ESSENTIALS
NEW YORK

Published in the United States by St. Martin's Essentials,
an imprint of St. Martin's Publishing Group

INTRODUCTION. Copyright © 2023 by Jon M. Sweeney. All rights reserved.
Printed in the United States of America. For information, address
St. Martin's Publishing Group, 120 Broadway, New York, NY 10271.

www.stmartins.com

The Library of Congress Cataloging-in-Publication Data is available upon request.

ISBN 978-1-250-87446-7 (trade paperback)
ISBN 978-1-250-87447-4 (ebook)

Our books may be purchased in bulk for promotional, educational, or business use.
Please contact your local bookseller or the Macmillan Corporate and
Premium Sales Department at 1-800-221-7945, extension 5442, or by
email at MacmillanSpecialMarkets@macmillan.com.

First St. Martin's Essentials Edition: 2023

10 9 8 7 6 5 4 3 2 1

This edition seeks to faithfully reproduce the original publications of the
author's works and so has maintained the original spelling and grammar throughout,
with only minor alterations for clarity or content.

Contents

Introduction by Jon M. Sweeney   1

Translator's Preface   7

BOOK I

PREPARATORY INSTRUCTIONS FOR THE SPIRITUAL LIFE

1. Of the Contempt of Worldly Vanities   37
2. Of Humility with Respect to Intellectual Attainments   39
3. Of the Knowledge of the Truth   41
4. Of Prudence with Respect to Our Opinions and Actions   45
5. Of Reading the Scriptures, and Other Holy Books   47
6. Of Inordinate Affections   49
7. Of Vain Hope, and Elation of Mind   51
8. Of Avoiding the Familiar Intercourses of the World   53
9. Of Subjection and Obedience   55

10.	Of Superfluous Talking	57
11.	Of True Peace of Mind, and Zeal for Spiritual Improvement	59
12.	Of the Benefit of Adversity	62
13.	Of Resisting Temptations	64
14.	Of Avoiding Rash Judgment	69
15.	Of Works of Charity	71
16.	Of Bearing the Infirmities of Others	73
17.	Of a Recluse Life	75
18.	Of the Examples of the Holy Fathers	77
19.	Of Religious Exercises	80
20.	Of Solitude and Silence	84
21.	Of Compunction of Heart	89
22.	Of the Consideration of Human Misery	92
23.	Of the Meditation of Death	96
24.	Of the Last Judgment, and the Punishment of Sinners	101
25.	Of Zeal in the Total Reformation of Life	105

BOOK II

INSTRUCTIONS FOR THE MORE INTIMATE
ENJOYMENT OF THE SPIRITUAL LIFE

1.	Of Internal Conversation	113
2.	Of Humble Submission to Reproof and Shame	118
3.	Of Peacefulness	122
4.	Of Simplicity and Purity	124
5.	Of Personal Attention	126

6. Of the Joy of a Good Conscience — 128

7. Of the Love of Jesus above All — 131

8. Of the Friendship of Jesus — 133

9. Of the Disconsolate State — 137

10. Of True Thankfulness for the Grace of God — 142

11. Of the Small Number of Those That Love the Cross — 145

12. Of the Necessity of Bearing the Cross — 148

BOOK III

OF DIVINE ILLUMINATION

1. Of the Blessedness of Internal Conversation
    with Christ — 157

2. That Christ, Who Is the Truth, Speaketh to the
    Soul, without the Sound of Words; That His
    Instructions Are to Be Heard with Humility; and
    That Many Regard Them Not — 159

3. The Soul Imploring the Influence of Grace, Is
    Instructed to Walk before God in Humility and
    Truth — 163

4. Of the Power of Divine Love — 167

5. Of the Trial of True Love — 171

6. That the Soul Must Not Despair under the Infirmities
    of Nature and the Suggestions of Evil Spirits — 172

7. Of Concealing the Grace of Devotion under the Veil
    of Humility — 175

8. That All Things Are to Be Referred to God, as the
    Ultimate End; and That the Service of God Is the
    Highest Honour, and the Most Perfect Freedom — 180

9. That the Good Desires of the Heart Are to Be
Carefully Examined and Regulated; and the Evil
Subdued by Continual Resistance   185

10. Of Meek Obedience, after the Example of Jesus
Christ; and of the Awful Consideration of the Divine
Judgments, as the Motive to an Humble Opinion
of Ourselves, and Our State in Grace   190

11. That Our Desires Must Be Expressed in Terms of
Absolute Resignation to the Divine Will   194

12. That True Comfort Is to Be Found Only in God   197

13. That, in Conformity to the Example of Christ,
the Miseries of This Fallen Life Are to Be Borne
with Patience and Resignation   200

14. Of Personal Infirmity, and the Miseries of the
Present Life   204

[15.] That the Soul Must Seek Her Repose
Only in God   207

15. That God Always Heareth the Prayer of
the Humble   209

16. Of the Thankful Remembrance of the Manifold
Mercies of God   212

17. Of Four Steps That Lead to Liberty and Peace   215

18. Of Avoiding a Curious Inspection into the Conduct
of Others   219

19. In What True Peace of Mind, and Spiritual
Perfection Consist   221

20. That Self-Love Is the Chief Obstruction to the
Attainment of the Supreme Good   225

21. That the Perverse Judgments, and Cruel Censures of Men, Are Not to Be Regarded 228

22. Of Submission to God in the Hour of Tribulation, and Confidence in Returning Grace 230

23. That the Creator Is to Be Found in Abstraction from the Creatures 235

24. Of Self-Denial, and the Renunciation of Animal Desire 238

25. Of the Instability of the Heart, and of Directing the Intention to God Alone 240

26. That the Soul Which Loves God, Enjoys Him in All Things, and above All; and in Him Findeth Peace 242

27. Against the Fear of Man 246

28. Perfect Freedom Can Only Be Attained by a Total Surrender of Self-Will 248

29. Of Self-Government in the Concerns of the Present Life, and of Having Recourse to God in All Its Difficulties and Dangers 251

30. Against Anxiety and Impetuosity in the Concerns of the World 253

31. That in Man There Is No Good; and That, Therefore, He Has Nothing in Which to Glory 255

32. Of the Contempt of All Temporal Honour, and the Renunciation of All Human Comfort 258

33. Of the Vanity of Human Learning 261

34. Of Disengagedness from the Business of the World, and the Opinions of Men 264

35. Of Credulity in the Promises and Professions of Men 266

36. Of Confidence in the Righteous Judgment of God,
    under the Various Accusations of Men   270

37. That All the Afflictions of the Present State Are to
    Be Patiently Endured for the Hope of Eternal Life   274

38. Of the Desire of Eternal Life, and of the Great
    Blessedness That Is Promised to Those Who
    Resolutely Strive to Obtain It   280

[38.] Of the Resignation of a Desolate Spirit to the
    Will of God   285

39. That When We Find Ourselves Incapable of the
    Higher Exercises of Devotion, We Should, with
    Humility, Practise the Lower; and Account Ourselves
    Rather Worthy of Affliction than Comfort   289

40. That the Grace of God Dwells Not with Those
    That Love the World   293

41. Of the Different Characters and Operations of
    Nature and Grace   296

42. That We Must Deny Ourselves, Take up the
    Cross of Christ, and Follow Him   305

43. Against Extravagant Dejection, upon Being
    Sometimes Betrayed by Human Weakness   308

44. Against the Vain and Presumptuous Inquiries
    of Reason into Subjects That Are above the
    Comprehension of the Natural Man   311

45. That All Hope and Confidence Is to Be Placed in
    God Alone   317

Introduction

One of my favorite stories of Thomas Merton, the famous twentieth-century monk and spiritual writer, is of the time before his conversion to Catholicism when he went to see the Bengali yogi and Hinduism scholar, Mahanambrata Brahmachari. Brahmachari was in New York City after having attended the World Festival of Faiths in Chicago, staying on to earn a doctorate at the University of Chicago before returning to India. Merton was a recent Columbia University graduate, questing and floundering. He asked the Hindu monk for recommendations of religious texts he might read.

Merton was familiar with Christianity, having been raised in a canopy sort of Anglicanism. "I became very fond of Brahmachari, and he of me. We got along very well together, especially since he sensed that I was trying to feel my way into a settled religious conviction, and into some kind of a life that was centered, as his was, on God," Merton wrote in his autobiography, *The Seven Storey Mountain.**

Brahmachari was prescient and wise. He told his young protege to look to the mystical classics in his own tradition rather than wander like a tourist into the religions of the East. Start with Augustine's *Confessions* and Thomas à Kempis's *The Imitation of Christ*, the scholar said. "You must read those books." It changed Merton's life.†

Perhaps Brahmachari learned to appreciate *The Imitation of Christ* from his Bengali elder, the groundbreaking Vivekananda, a disciple of Ramakrishna, who introduced Hinduism and Vedanta to the West in 1893 at the Parliament of the Religions, in the building on Michigan Avenue that's now the Art Institute of Chicago. Vivekananda loved and translated *The Imitation of Christ* into Bengali in 1899. He wrote in his introduction to that translation of the parallels between *The Imitation* and the most important scripture of his own tradition, the *Bhagavad Gita.*‡ Both texts, he said, were songs of God.

I also remember how Thomas à Kempis, the author of *The Imitation of Christ*, impacted lives of other literary and philosophical luminaries, even some more notorious characters. England's King Henry VIII, for instance, was known to praise Kempis's book, even though its message of love seems to have been lost on him in action. The last of his six wives, Catherine Parr, summarized the principles and prayers of *The Imitation* in her own

---

* Thomas Merton, *The Seven Storey Mountain* (New York: Harcourt, Brace and Company, 1948), 195.

† Merton, *The Seven Storey Mountain*, 198.

‡ Amiya P. Sen, *Explorations in Modern Bengal c. 1800–1900: Essays on Religion, History and Culture* (Delhi: Primus Books, 2010), 208.

Prayers or Meditations, the first book in English by a woman published under her own name, in 1545. In the English colonies of the New World, Kempis was published in Germantown (Maryland) twenty-seven years before the Revolution.

The Imitation of Christ once formed people the way that Bible reading did. The great atheist philosopher, Bertrand Russell was under its sway as a young man, before he found his atheist convictions. Russell's exact contemporary across the Channel, Marie Françoise-Thérèse Martin (they were born just eight months apart), was under its sway too. Russell would soon discover Spinoza, instead, while Thérèse Martin committed long passages of Kempis to memory, quoting them in times of need, and incorporating the teachings into her own great work, *The Story of a Soul.* Thérèse we know today as St. Thérèse of Lisieux.

Around the same time, Leo Tolstoy was spending an increasing amount of time with Kempis in Russia, finding more in the obscure German-Dutch master's little book than in the stories that had already made Tolstoy famous throughout the world. One hint of Kempis's influence on the great novelist appears in book five, chapter three of *War and Peace:* "On reaching Petersburg Pierre did not let anyone know of his arrival, he went nowhere and spent whole days reading Thomas à Kempis, whose book had been sent to him by someone unknown. One thing he continually realized as he read that book: the joy, hitherto unknown to him, of believing in the possibility of attaining perfection and in the possibility of active brotherly love among men."*

"The joy . . . of believing in the possibility of attaining per-

---

* Tolstoy, *War and Peace,* trans. Louise and Aylmer Maude (New York: Oxford University Press, 1942), vol. 1, 469.

fection and in the possibility of active brotherly love." That's the appeal of this classic work. Is this possible in human life?

They say *The Imitation of Christ* has been read by more people than any other book but the Bible, since first appearing in manuscript copies in about 1425. Kempis wrote and published it anonymously. He intended his book to be a series of devotional and mystical explanations and applications of what is found in the New Testament gospels and epistles. Those ideas about perfection and love began there. If it's really possible, how?

In one of the notebooks found after his death, Franz Kafka jotted, "Everyone carries a room about inside them."[*] He understood what Kempis did, that perhaps this perfection is more real inside of us than when we go out into the world. Similarly, the Jesuit priest and paleontologist Pierre Teilhard de Chardin once said, "At the heart of our universe, each soul exists for God, in our Lord."[†] That's the easy part—in the soul. What about when we are with other people?

Kempis's message is that humility is essential, and real trust in God is possible. Witness this quote from Book Three: "If I humble myself to nothingness, if I shrink from all self-esteem and account myself as the dust which I am, Your grace will favor me, Your light will enshroud my heart. . . . I am nothing but total weakness. But if You look upon me for an instant, I am at once made strong and filled with new joy." As a twenty-first century person who still turns to this fifteenth-century spiritual classic, I want to help you hear this in a context of relevance.

---

[*] Kafka, *Wedding Preparation in the Country and Other Posthumous Prose Writings,* with notes by Max Brod, trans. Ernest Kaiser and Eithne Wilkins (London: Secker and Warburg, 1954), 54.

[†] Teilhard, *The Divine Milieu* (New York: Harper & Row, 1960), 56.

We worry about so much, and for good reason. We face so much danger. So we occupy ourselves with distractions, to avoid thinking or feeling too much. This shared anxiety is the context for Kempis's book. He wants you not to resign, but to engage more deeply. He summarizes this early on, succinctly: "Sorrow opens the door to many a blessing which dissoluteness usually destroys."*

Kempis is reminding us not to let the world have a grip on us. To not allow the suffering and vicissitudes to control us. To remain steadfast in the knowledge and experience of God, whose love is within us.

Next, he points and pushes us to be where we need to be to see, hear, and understand this divine love. For instance, be deliberate with your life by recognizing that one day you will die. "The present is very precious; these are the days of salvation; now is the acceptable time."† Zeal and diligence, too, come highly recommended. This is a book designed to challenge every spiritual underachiever. And all of this is before we get to the meat of Kempis's teaching in Books Two and Three, where he advises on how to have and cultivate an interior life.

Meditation and peace. Achieving purity of mind. Finding the joy of a clear conscience. Friendship with Jesus, who knows our suffering. Hearing truth that speaks without words in our souls. We need these lessons as much as any human beings ever have.

Rereading *The Imitation of Christ* now, and remembering how I first read it at the age of eighteen, I'm reminded that we read

---

* See the chapter "Sorrow of Heart."

† See the chapter "Thoughts on Death."

differently depending on our stage in life. At eighteen, I did not love the world the way I do at fifty-five. At eighteen, I didn't see how ethics and spiritual practice are more important than theology. The primary theme of *The Imitation of Christ* is conversion, and that's the work of a lifetime, and the duty of every person who wants to be a decent human being.

—Jon M. Sweeney is a Catholic, rabbi spouse, editor, and author. He's written many books including *Thomas Merton* (St. Martin's Essentials) and *Feed the Wolf.*

Translator's Preface

As "The Christian's Pattern," by Dean Stanhope, has claimed a place among the translations of this excellent book, and by an implicit admission has obtained general approbation; it will undoubtedly be asked, what occasion there was for attempting a new one? And to this question, no other answer, as an apology for the translation that is now offered to the public, can be given, than that it was attempted in the hope of doing some justice to the sense of the original; which is almost lost in the loose paraphrase of Dean Stanhope, and almost deprived of its spirit, by the literal and inelegant exactness of others.

With what degree of success this attempt has been prosecuted, must be left wholly to the judgment of the reader. It is hoped, however, that, where the original allowed of some latitude in the translation, no sense is introduced, that will not be found coincident with the author's great principle, "The necessity of exchanging an earthly for a heavenly nature;" and that an apology will not be required, for giving the preference, in several instances of competition, to some apposite passage in the Divine oracles, as the best illustration of the thought, and the most forcible manner of expressing it. As this preference has been given, wherever an occasion was supposed to offer, the quotations from the sacred Scriptures are more numerous than they are in the original: and though all the quotations in the original are taken from the Vulgate Bible, yet here they are generally taken from our English Bible; and the Vulgate is seldom retained, but where the force of the author's sentiment depended upon the peculiar turn given to that translation.

In the third book, the division and the titles of the chapters are different, not only from all the translations, but from all the editions of the original that have been consulted upon this occasion, except the late Paris edition, published by M. J. Valart; which, as it is declared to have been formed upon an accurate collation of manuscripts, and old printed copies; and, in consequence of that collation, purified from more than six hundred errors, has been chosen as the standard with respect to this translation.

Of the book itself, it will be difficult to show the excellency and use, to those that have no sense of spiritual devotion; and unnecessary, to those that have. The numerous editions of the original, however, and the numerous translations of it into the different languages of all the nations professing Christianity, whether as Protestants or Papists, that have been continually published for near three hundred years, is a testimony of approbation which few human compositions can boast; and which the advocates for libertinism, though they may pretend to despise it, cannot but secretly venerate.

But, besides the professors and patrons of profane wit, and

unrestrained pleasure, there are some sober minds, who, because they live in a nation where Christianity is professed, have assumed the character of Christians; and being perfectly pleased with themselves, and satisfied with following the regular rotation of formal duties, are offended at every attempt to convince them, that "there is something still needful" of much higher importance than the most minute conformity to the ceremonials of external worship. They have also assumed the character of Protestants—an honourable character, if formed upon Christian principles, and supported with a Christian spirit!—and when motives to the attainment of a divine life, urged by a Roman Catholic, are offered to their consideration, their displeasure is heightened; and the offer is rejected, not only with indignation, but with a dread of all the evils which they have been used to associate with the idea of a Roman Catholic. Like those of old, who asked, "if anything good could come out of Nazareth;" they are ready to exclaim, "Can precepts of truth and holiness proceed from the cell of a monk?" And no less danger is apprehended, than that of being artfully betrayed into the trammels of a spiritual director: or artfully worked up to such a rage of ill-humour with themselves and the world, as to be driven into the irremeable gate of a cloister.

The author of this book had no design that terminates in any of the changeable forms and perishing interests of the present life. As a Roman Catholic he has himself performed the office of a spiritual director; and it is to bring and leave his disciple, where he leaves himself, under the conduct of the only guide to life, light, holiness, and peace, the Spirit of God. In his own person he makes this address: "O God, who art the Truth, make me one with thee in everlasting love! I am often weary of reading, and weary of hearing: in thee alone is the sum of my desires! Let all teachers be silent; let the whole creation be dumb before thee; and do thou only speak unto my soul!"* And in another place, in the character of that disciple of whom he has been the director, he says: "Speak, Lord; for thy servant heareth. Let not Moses speak to me, nor any of the prophets. But do thou, O Lord my God, Eternal truth! Speak to my soul; lest, being only outwardly warned, but not inwardly quickened, I die and be found unfruitful; lest the word heard, and not obeyed, known and not loved, professed and not kept, turn to my condemnation! Speak, therefore, Lord, for thy servant heareth: Thou only, hast the words of eternal life! O speak to the comfort of my soul, to the renovation of my heavenly nature, and to the eternal praise and glory of thy own holy name."†

As a Roman Catholic also, he had renounced the world, and devoted his time and attention to the purification of his spirit, in the retirement of a cloister: and even in a cloister, he frequently deplores the worldly and sensual life of many that were immured with him; and directs man to a more sacred retirement, his own heart, to discover the evil of his fallen nature, and the manifestations of that divine power, which is his only redemption from it. It is the renunciation of the spirit of the world, and a continual dependance upon the Spirit of God, as the principle of all truth and goodness, that are the duties he enjoins, and the perfection he requires; and if this perfection is attained in the midst of the tumultuous scenes of life, it can suffer no abatement, because it was not attained in the retirement of a cloister. What he sought himself in a state of retirement, he tells us in these words: "It is

---

* Book I. Chap. iii. § 3.

† Book III. Chap. ii. § 2, 3.

not the peculiar habit, the tonsure, or any alteration merely external, but a change of heart, and an entire mortification of the passions, that are the indispensable qualifications for such a state; and he that seeks anything in it, but the glory of God in the purification of his own soul, will meet only with disappointment and trouble, anxiety and remorse."*

Retirement into a cloister, is not a precept of the Christian faith; but the renunciation of the world, is one of its essential duties; and universally enjoined, as an indispensable condition of becoming faithful followers of Him who, as our Exampler, as well as our Redeemer, had himself renounced and overcome the world; and if this duty had been universally fulfilled by those who have assumed the sacred character of his faithful followers, retirement into a cloister would never have been known.

But we are to consider, what has been the state of Christianity since it became national; and how deplorably all Christian nations have fallen from the spirit and power of the Gospel of Christ. What has any Christian nation ever aimed at, but an emulation of the wealth and splendour, the policy, the luxury, the refined vanity, the pride, pomp, and power of Pagan Greece and Rome? What does any Christian nation now seek, but even to outdo Pagan Greece and Rome, in all the frantic excesses of a worldly spirit; devoting all the faculties of an immortal soul, and all the short time of its probation for eternity, to the diversification of the scenes of sensual pleasure, or to the accumulation of poisonous riches, which become proportionably more deadly, the more they are collected and engrossed; violating the sacred obligations of justice and charity, to seize each other's posses-

---

* Book 1. Chap. xvii. § 2.

sions; and calling in the aid of hell, to secure the plunder with every murdering engine of war? Now he, who, in such a state of Christianity, labours to fulfil the precept, and follow the example of his Redeemer, in the renunciation and conquest of the world, will find that he must labour in an abstraction, not less painful in itself, nor less unfriendly to worldly interest, than retirement into a cloister, in whatever formidable light his imagination may have painted it.

If we did not know what men may do and say, with the gospel in their hands, and the Sun of Righteousness still shedding his vital beams upon them, we should wonder—that those who at their baptism, have "solemnly renounced the world, the flesh and the devil;" and who in the public service of the church, hear the precepts of their Redeemer, "to overcome the world, deny themselves, take up their daily cross, and follow Him;" and in the use of its liturgy, repeat the most earnest prayers for "the continual influences of the Holy Spirit, to enable them to fulfil those precepts, because they cannot do it by their own strength,"—we should wonder that such persons should be the most violent in exclaiming against books like this, as the ravings of enthusiasm, or the dreams of monkish ignorance, because they call men to "the renunciation of the world, self-denial, watchfulness and prayer, and to a continual unreserved dependance upon the illuminating and sanctifying influences of the Holy Spirit."

The author had a profound knowledge of the spiritual life; such as is not to be acquired, but by a mind truly devoted, and long inured, to spiritual exercises. He stops not at calling men to the renunciation of the world, self-denial, watchfulness, and prayer; but leads them on to that naked faith, absolute resignation, and pure love, which are the strength and beauty of the regenerate nature—the nature which can alone enter into heaven, because it comes out of heaven: that can alone love, desire, and unite with God, because it is born of God! His instructions, therefore, are founded upon this great principle, which is also the foundation of the precepts of the Gospel—that "man has lost the divine life born of God, and is fallen into an earthly, animal, and sensual life of this world; a life of darkness, impurity, impotence, and misery; which must be abandoned, that his first divine life may be regenerated in him by the operation of the Holy Ghost." And as it would be in vain to offer such instructions, to those who think they do not want them; so it is in vain, that Christ once preached to men himself, and has continued preaching to them by his Holy Spirit, while they shun, or disguise, or misapply everything, that would bring them to a sense of the darkness, impurity, impotence and misery, of their life in this world.

Men, in their fallen state, are destitute of happiness, restless and insatiable in their desires of it, and always seeking it, where it cannot possibly be found, in themselves, and their earthly life: and men, in these days of fallen Christianity are only in a better state, because some real, though alienated goodness, is produced by the efforts of that Divine life, which is struggling for redemption within them. They know their Master has declared that "there is but one who is good, and that is God;" and yet, they know not, or will not know, that whatever goodness lives in intelligent natures, from the highest angel to the lowest of mankind, is solely the manifestation of the presence and power of Him, who alone is good. All the light and goodness, therefore, which the mercy of God, notwithstanding their repugnancy, still preserves within them, as their call to heaven, they arrogate as the light of human reason, and the attainments of human virtue; and confiding wholly in themselves, and contented with the forms of godliness instead of the power, they stifle the sense of their inherent darkness, impurity, impotence, and misery, by mingling in the cares and pleasures of a vain and busy world. But they are questions that deserve the most serious consideration, whether Christ is not the Saviour of men, only by being formed within them, as the living power of knowing and fulfilling the will of God: and whether those that reject him as this inward Saviour, who alone, by the manifestation of his own nature, life and spirit in the soul, can transform selfish, sensúal, proud, and malignant spirits, into angels of patience, humility, meekness, purity, and love, and from "children of wrath," make them "children of the living God;" reject him less than the Scribes and Pharisees, who blasphemed, persecuted, and put him to death.

"Some," says the author, speaking in the person of Christ, "place their religion in books; some, in images; and some, in the pomp and splendor of external worship: these honor me with their lips, but their heart is far from me. But there are some who, with illuminated understandings, discern the glory which man has lost, and with pure affections pant for its recovery: these hear and speak, with reluctance, of the cares and pleasures of the present life, and even lament the necessity of administering to the wants of animal nature: these hear and understand what the Holy Spirit speaketh in their heart; exhorting them, to withdraw their affection from things on earth, and set it on things above; to abandon this fallen world, and day and night aspire after re-union with God."*

---

* Book III. Chap. iii. § 8.

As the fittest key to unlock the treasures of this inestimable book, and lay them open to common use, it may be necessary to show, in general, the ground and nature of Christian redemption; and it can scarcely be done with more power of conviction, than in the following extracts from the writings of a great divine, whose name is not mentioned, because names have been known to endear error, and to keep the eyes shut from the sight of truth.

The fall of man into the life and state of this world, is the whole ground of his redemption; and a real birth of Christ in the soul, is the whole nature of it. To convince man of his fall, as the ground of his redemption, it is not necessary to appeal to the history which Moses has given of it; because Moses's history of the fall, is not the proof of it; and because a mere historical knowledge of the fall, would not do man any real good. Moses has recorded the death of the first man, and of many of his descendants: but the proof that man is mortal, lies not in Moses's history, but in the known nature of man, and the world from which he has his life. Thus, though Moses has recorded the time and manner of the fall, yet there is no more occasion to have recourse to his history to prove it, than to prove that man is a poor, weak, vain, distressed, corrupt, depraved, selfish, self-tormenting, perishing creature; and that the world is a sad mixture of imaginary good, and real evil, a mere scene of vanity, vexation, and misery. This is the known nature and condition, both of man and the world; and every man is, in himself, an irresistible proof that he is in a fallen state. An attempt, therefore, to convince man of his fall, as the ground of his redemption, must be an attempt to do that which misfortunes, sickness, pain, and the approach of death, have a natural tendency to do; to convince him of the vanity, poverty, and misery of his life and condition in this world; and how impossible it is, that a God, who has nothing in himself but infinite goodness, and infinite happiness, should bring forth a race of intelligent creatures, that have neither natural goodness, nor natural happiness.

Man, in his first state, as he came forth from God, must have been absolutely free from all vanity, want, or distress, of any kind, from anything either within or without him: a God-like perfection of nature, and a painful, distressed nature, stand in the utmost contrariety to one another. But man has lost his first divine life in God; everything that we know of God, and everything that we know of man, of his birth, his life, and death, is a continual irresistible proof, that man is in a fallen state. The human infant, just come out of the womb, is a picture of such deformity, nakedness, weakness, and helpless distress, as is not to be found among the home-born animals of this world. The chicken has its birth from no sin, and therefore, comes forth in beauty; it runs and pecks, as soon as its shell is broken: the calf and the lamb go both to play, as soon as the dam is delivered of them; they are pleased with themselves, and please the eye that beholds their frolicsome state, and beauteous clothing: while the new-born babe of a woman, that is to have an upright form; that is to view the heavens, and worship that God that made him lies, for months, in gross ignorance, weakness, and impurity; as sad a spectacle, when he first breathes the life of this world, as when in the agonies of death he breathes his last. What is all this, but the strongest proof, that man is the only creature that belongs not to this world, but is fallen into it through sin; and that, therefore, his birth, in such distress, bears all these marks of shame and weakness? Had he been originally of this world, this world would have done the highest honour to its highest creature; and he must have begun his life in greater perfection than any other animal, and brought with him a more beautiful clothing than the finest lilies of the field. But when the human infant has at length acquired strength, and begins to act for himself, he soon becomes a more pitiable object than when crying in the cradle. The strength of his life, is a mere strength of wild passions; his reason is craft and selfish subtlety; he loves and hates only as flesh and blood prompt him; and jails and gibbets cannot keep him from theft and murder. If he is rich, he is tormented with pride and ambition; if poor, with want and discontent; be he which he will, sooner or later, disordered passions, disappointed lusts, fruitless labour, pains and sickness, will tear him from this world, in such travail as his mother felt, when she brought forth the sinful animal. Now all this evil and misery are the natural and necessary effect of his birth in the bestial flesh and blood of this world; and there is nothing in his natural state, that can put a stop to it; he must be evil and miserable, as long as he has only the life of this world in him. Therefore the absolute certainty of man's fall, and the absolute necessity of a new birth to redeem him, are truths, independently of Scripture, plain to a demonstration.

No creature can come from the hands of God, into a state of any ignorance of anything that is proper to be known by it; this is as impossible, as for God to have an envious or evil will. Now all right and natural knowledge, in whatever creature it is, is sensible, intuitive, and its own evidence; and opinion, reasoning, or doubting, can only then begin, when the creature has lost its first right and natural state, and has got somewhere, and become somewhat, that it cannot tell what to make of.

Reasoning, doubting, and perplexity, in any creature, are the effect of some fall or departure from its first state of nature; and show, that it wants, and is seeking, something that belongs to its nature, but knows not how to come at it. The beasts seek not after truth; a plain proof, that it has no relation to them, no suitableness to their nature, nor ever belonged to them. Man is in quest of it, in perplexity about it, cannot come at it; takes lies to be truth, and truth to be lies: a plain proof, both that he has it not, and yet has had it; was created in it, and for it; for no creature can seek for anything, but that which has been lost, and is wanted; nor could man form the least idea of it, but because it has belonged to him, and ought to be his.

Now suppose man to come into the world, with this chief difference from other creatures, that he is at a loss to find out what he is, how he is to live, and what he is to seek as his chief happiness; what he is to own of a God, of providence, religion, &c., suppose him to have faculties that put him upon this search, and no faculties that can satisfy his inquiry; and what can we suppose more miserable in himself, and more unworthy of a good Creator? Therefore, if we will not suppose, that God has been good to all creatures, and given every animal its proper light of nature, except man; we must be forced to own, that man has lost the true light and perfection of his nature, which God at first gave him.

God is, in himself, infinite truth, infinite goodness, and infinite happiness; but man, in his present earthly birth and life, has neither truth, goodness nor happiness; therefore, his present state of life could not be brought forth by that God, who is all truth, goodness, and happiness. Thus every man, that believes in a Creator infinitely perfect, is under a necessity of believing the whole ground of Christian redemption, namely, that man has lost that perfection of life, which he had at first from his Creator,

Had not a divine life at first been in man, he would be now at the same distance from truth and goodness, and as incapable of forming the least thought or desire of them, as the beasts of the field; and would have nothing to do, but to look to himself, live to his earthly nature, and make the most of this world; for this is all the wisdom and goodness that an earthly nature is capable of, whether it be a man or a fox. The certainty of the fact, of man's first divine life, is all; nothing more need be inquired after: for on this ground stands all his comfort; hence it is, that in faith and hope he can look up to God as his father, to heaven as his native country, and on himself as a stranger and a pilgrim upon earth.

For it is a certain truth, that fallen, earthly, and corrupt, as human nature is, there is, in the soul of every man, the fire, and light, and love of God, though lodged in a state of hiddenness and inactivity, till something human or divine, distress or grace, or both, discover its life within us.

We were no more created to be in the sorrows, burdens, and anguish of this earthly life, than the angels were created to be in the wrath and darkness of hell. It is as contrary to the will and goodness of God toward us, that we are out of paradise, as it is contrary to the designs and goodness of God towards the angels, that some of them are out of heaven, prisoners of darkness. How absurd, and even blasphemous would it be, to say, with the church and the scriptures, that "we are children of wrath, and born in sin," if we had that nature which God at first gave us? What a reproach upon God, to say, that this world is a valley of misery, a shadow of death, full of disorders, sorrows, and temptations, if this was an original creation, or that state of things in which God created us? Is it not as consistent with the goodness of God, to speak of the misery and disorder that holy angels find above, and of the sorrows and vanity of their heavenly state, as to speak of the misery of men, and the sorrows and vanity of this world, if men and the world were in that order, in which God at first had placed them? If God could make any place poor and vain, and create any beings into a state of vanity and vexation of spirit, he might do so in all places, and to all beings.

The fall of man, therefore, into the life of this earthly world, is the sole ground of his wanting the redemption which the gospel offers. Hence it is, that the gospel has only one simple proposal of certain life, or certain death, to man: of life, if he will take the means of entering into the kingdom of God; of death, if he chooses to take up his rest in the kingdom of this world. This is the simple nature, and sole drift of the gospel; it means no more, than making known to man, that this world, and the life of it, is his fall and separation from God and happiness, both here and hereafter; and that to be saved, or restored to God and happiness, can only be obtained, by renouncing all love and adherence to the things of this world. All the precepts, threatenings and doctrines of the gospel, mean nothing, but to drive all earthly-mindedness and carnal affections out of the soul; to call man from the life, spirit, and goods of this world, to a life of faith and hope, and love and desire of a new birth from heaven.

To embrace the gospel, is to enter, with all our hearts, into its terms of dying to all that is earthly, both within us and without us: and, on the other hand, to place our faith, and hope, and trust, and satisfaction, in the things of this world, is to reject the gospel, with our whole heart, spirit and strength, as much as any infidel can do, notwithstanding we make ever so many verbal assents to everything that is recorded in the New Testament.

This, therefore, is the one true, essential distinction, between the Christian and the Infidel. The Infidel is a man of this world, wholly devoted to it; his hope and faith are set upon it; for where our heart is, there, and there only, are our hope and faith: he has only such a virtue, such a goodness, and such a religion, as entirely suits with the interests of flesh and blood, and keeps the soul happy in "the lust of the flesh, the lust of the eye, and the pride of life." This, and this alone, is Infidelity; a total separation from God, and a removal of all faith and hope from him, into the life of this world. It matters not, whether this Infidel be a professor of the gospel, a disciple of Zoroaster, a follower of Plato, a Jew, a Turk, or an opposer of the gospel history: this difference of opinions or professions alters not the matter; it is the love of the world instead of God, that constitutes the whole nature of the Infidel.

On the other hand, the Christian renounces the world as his horrid prison; he dies to the will of flesh and blood, because it is darkness, corruption, and separation from God; he turns from all that is earthly, animal and temporal, and stands in a continual tendency of faith and hope, and prayer to God, to have a better nature, a better life and spirit, born again into him from above.

Where this faith is, there is the Christian, the "new creature in Christ, born of the Word and Spirit of God:" neither time nor place, nor any outward condition of birth and life, can hinder his entrance into the kingdom of God. But where this faith is not, there is the true complete Infidel, "the man of the earth," the unredeemed, the rejecter of the gospel, "the son of perdition," that is "dead in trespasses and sins, without Christ, an alien from the commonwealth of Israel, a stranger to the covenants of promise, having no hope, and without God in the world."

Men are apt to consider a worldly spirit only as an infirmity, or pardonable failure; but it is, indeed, the great apostacy from God and the divine life: it is not a single sin, but the whole nature of all sin; that leaves no possibility of coming out of our fallen state, till it be totally renounced with all the strength of our hearts.

Our Lord says, there is but one that is good, and that is God." In the same strictness of expression it must be said, "there is but one life that is good, and that is the life of God and heaven." Depart, in the least degree, from the goodness of God, and you depart into evil; because nothing is good, but his goodness. Choose any life, but the life of God and heaven, and you choose death; for death is nothing else but the loss of the life of God. The creatures of this world have but one life, and one good, and that is the life of this world: eternal beings have but one life, and one good, and that is the life of God. The spirit of the soul is in itself nothing else but a spirit breathed forth from God, that the life of God, the nature of God, the working of God, the tempers of God, might be manifested in it. God could not create man to have a will of his own, and a life of his own, different from the life and will that is in himself; this is more impossible than for a good tree to bring forth corrupt fruit. God can only delight in his own life, his own goodness, and his own perfections; and, therefore, cannot love or delight, or dwell in any creatures, but where his own goodness and perfections are to be found: like can only unite with like, heaven with heaven, and hell with hell; and, therefore, the life of God must be the life of the soul, if the soul is to unite with God. Hence it is, that all the religion of fallen man, all the methods of our redemption, have only this one end to take from us that strange and earthly life we have gotten by the fall, and to kindle again the life of God and heaven in our souls: not to deliver us from that gross and sordid vice called covetousness which heathens can condemn; but to take the spirit of this world entirely from us.

This spirit is the whole nature and misery of our fall; it keeps our souls in a state of death; and, as long as it governs, makes it impossible for us to be "born again from above." It is the greatest blindness and darkness of our nature, and keeps us in the grossest ignorance both of heaven and hell; for though they are both of them within us, yet we feel neither, while the spirit of this world reigns in us. Light and truth, and the gospel, so far as they concern eternity, are all empty sounds to the wordly spirit: his own good and his own evil, govern all his hopes and fears; and, therefore, he can have no religion, or be farther concerned in it, than so far as it can be made serviceable to the life of this world: he can know nothing of God, for he can know nothing, feel nothing, taste nothing, delight in nothing, but with earthly senses, and after an earthly manner. "The natural man," saith the apostle "receiveth not the things of the Spirit of God; they are foolishness unto him: he cannot know them, because they are spiritually discerned;" that is, they can only be discerned by that spirit, which he hath not: he can only contemplate them, as things foreign to himself; as so many changeable ideas, which he receives from books or hearsay, and which become a bad nourishment of all his natural tempers: he is proud of his ability to discourse about them, and loses all humility, all love of God and man, through a vain and haughty contention for them. He stands at the same distance from a living perception of the truth, as the man that is born blind, does from a living perception of light; light must first be the birth of his own life, before he can enter into a real knowledge of it.

The measure of our life, is the measure of our knowledge; and as the spirit of our life worketh, so the spirit of our understanding conceiveth. If our will worketh with God, though our natural capacity be ever so mean and narrow, we get a real knowledge of God, and heavenly truth; for every thing must feel that in which it lives. But if our will worketh with Satan, and the spirit of this world, let our parts be ever so bright, our imaginations ever so soaring; yet all our living knowledge can go no higher or deeper, than the mysteries of iniquity, and the lusts of flesh and blood. For nothing feels, or tastes, or understands, or likes, or dislikes, but the life that is in us: the spirit that leads our life, is the spirit that forms our understanding. The mind is our eye, and all the faculties of the mind see every thing according to the state the mind is in. If selfish pride is the spirit of our life, every thing is only seen, and known thro'this glass; every thing is dark, senseless, and absurd, to the proud man, but that which brings food to this spirit: he understands nothing, feels nothing, but as his pride is made sensible of it, or capable of being affected with it. His working will, which is the life of his soul, liveth and worketh only in the element of pride; and, therefore, what suits his pride, is his only good; and what contradicts his pride, is all the evil that he can feel or know: his wit, his parts, his learning, his advancement, his friends, his admirers, his successes, his conquests, all these are the only god and heaven, that he has any living perception of: he indeed can talk of a Scripture God, a

Scripture Christ, and heaven: but these are only the ornamental furniture of his brain, whilst pride is the god of his heart. We are told, that "God resisteth the proud, and giveth grace to the humble." This is not to be understood, as if God, by an arbitrary will only chose to deal thus with the proud and humble man. But the true ground is this; the resistance is on the part of man. Pride resisteth God, it rejecteth him, it turneth from him, and chooseth to worship and adore something else instead of him: whereas humility leaveth all for God, falls down before him, and opens the whole heart to receive him. This is the only sense, in which "God resisteth the proud, and giveth grace to the humble." And thus it is in the true ground of every good and evil that rises up in us; we have neither good nor evil, but as it is the natural effect of the working of our own will, either with, or against, God. Consider the state of him, whose working will is under the power of wrath; he sees, and hears, and feels, and understands, and talks, wholly from the light and sense of wrath; all his faculties are only so many faculties of wrath; and he has no sense or knowledge, but what his enlightened wrath discovers to him. These instances are sufficient to show, that the state of our life governs the state of our mind, and forms the degree and manner of our understanding and knowledge; and that, therefore, there is no possibility of knowing God and divine truth, till our life is divine, and wholy dead to the life and spirit of this world.

"The philosophers of old began all their virtue, in a total renunciation of the spirit of this world. They saw, with the eyes of heaven, that darkness was not more contrary to light, than the wisdom of this world was contrary to the spirit of virtue: therefore, they allowed of no progress in virtue, but so far as a man had overcome himself, and the spirit of this world. This gave a divine solidity to all their instructions, and proved them to be masters of true wisdom. But the doctrine of the Cross of Christ, the last, the highest, the finishing stroke given to the spirit of this world, that speaks more in one word than all the philosophy of voluminous writers, is yet professed by those who are in more friendship with the world, than was allowed to the disciples of Pythagoras, Socrates, Plato, or Epictetus. Nay, if those ancient sages were to start up amongst us with their divine wisdom, they would bid fair to be treated by the sons of the gospel, if not by some fathers of the church, as dreaming enthusiasts. But it is a standing truth, that "the world can only love its own, and wisdom can only be justified of her children." The heaven-born Epictetus told one of his scholars, that "then he might first look upon himself as having made some proficiency in virtue, when the world took him for a fool;" an oracle like that which said, "the wisdom of this world is foolishness with God."

If it be asked, "What is the apostacy of these last times, or whence is the degeneracy of the present Christian church?" it is all the progeny of a worldly spirit. If here we see open wickedness, there only forms of godliness; if here superficial holiness, political piety, crafty prudence; there haughty sanctity, partial zeal, envious orthodoxy; if, almost everywhere, we find a Jewish blindness and hardness of heart, and the church trading with the gospel, as visibly as the old Jews bought and sold beasts in their temple; all this is only so many forms and proper fruits of the worldly spirit. This is the great chain with which the devil enslaves mankind; and every son of man is held captive in it, till through, and by the Spirit of Christ, he breaks from it. Nothing else can deliver him from it: nothing leaves the world, nothing renounces it, nothing can possibly overcome it, but the Spirit of Christ. Hence it is, that many learned men, with all the rich furniture of their brain, live and die slaves to the spirit of this world, and can only differ from gross worldlings, as the Scribes and Pharisees differed from publicans and sinners: it is because the Spirit of Christ is not the one only thing that is the desire of their hearts; and, therefore, their learning only works in and with the spirit of this world, and becomes itself no small part of the "vanity of vanities."

"Nothing does, or can, keep God out of the soul, or hinder his holy union with it, but its desire turned from him:" for with whatever the will worketh, with that only the soul liveth, whether it be God or the creature. Whatever the soul desireth, that is the fuel of its fire; and as its fuel is, so is the flame of its life. A will given up to earthly enjoyments, is at grass with Nebuchadnezzar, and has one life with the beasts of the field; for earthly desires keep up the same life in a man and an ox. For the one only reason why the animals of this world have no sense or knowledge of God, is because they cannot form any other than earthly desires, and so can only have an earthly life: when, therefore, a man wholly turneth his will to earthly desires, he dies to the excellency of his natural state, and may be said only to live, and move, and have his being in the life of this world, as the beasts have. Earthly food, &c., only desired and used for the support of the earthly body, is suitable to man's present condition, and the order of nature: but when the desires and delight of the soul are set upon earthly things, the humanity is degraded, is fallen from God; and the life of the soul is made as earthly and bestial as the life of the body; for the creature can be neither higher nor lower, neither better nor worse, than as its will worketh. What it desireth, that it taketh; and of that it eateth and liveth; wherever, and in whatever, the will chooseth to dwell and delight, that becometh the soul's food, its condition, its body, its clothing, and habitation. Nothing doth, nor can, go with a man into heaven, nothing followeth him into hell, but that in which the will dwelt, with which it was fed, nourished, and clothed, in this life. Death can make no alteration of this state of the will; it only takes off the outward worldly covering of flesh and blood, and forces the soul to see, and feel, and know, what a life, what a state, food, body, and habitation, its own working will has brought forth for it. Is there, therefore, any thing in life that deserves a thought, but how to keep this working of our will in a right state, and to get that purity of heart, which alone can see, and know, and find and possess God? Is there any thing so frightful as this worldly spirit, which turns the soul from God, makes it a house of darkness, and feeds it with the food of time, at the expense of all the riches of eternity?

Now, as the whole nature of the gospel redemption means nothing, but the one true, and only possible way, of delivering man from all the evil of his fall—a fall demonstrable to the senses and understanding of every man, by every height and depth of nature; by every kind of evil, sin and misery in the world; by every thing he knows of God, himself, and the world he lives in. Christianity is not only the desirable thing that the heart of man can think of, but the most intelligible, and self-evident. It requires not the aid of learning for its support; it stands upon a foundation superior to human learning, and may be the sure possession of every plain man, who has sense enough to know, whether he is happy or unhappy, good or evil. For this natural knowledge, if adhered to, is every man's sure guide to that one salvation preached by the gospel; which gospel stands in no more need of learning and critical art now, than it did when Christ was preaching it upon earth. How absurd would it have been, for any critics in Greek and Hebrew, to have followed Christ and his apostles, as necessary explainers of their words, which called for nothing in the hearers, but penitent hearts turned to God; and declared that "they only who were of God, could hear the word of God!" If none but learned men have the true fitness to understand the word of scripture, and the plain man is to receive it from them, how must he know, which are the scholars that have the right knowledge? Whence is he to have his information? For no one need be told, that ever since learning has borne rule in the church, learned doctors have contradicted and condemned each other, in every essential point of the Christian doctrine. Thousands of learned men tell the illiterate, they are lost in this or that church; and thousands of learned men tell them, they are lost if they leave it. If, therefore, Christianity is in the hands of scholars, how must the plain man come at it? Must he, though unable to understand scripture for want of learning, tell which learned man is in the right, and which is not? If so, the unlearned man must have far the greatest ability, since he is to do that for scholars, which they cannot do for themselves.

But Christian redemption is God's mercy to all mankind, and every fallen man, as such, has a fitness or capacity to lay hold of it. It has no dependance upon times and places, or the ages and several conditions of the world, or any outward circumstances of life; as the first man partook of it, so must the last: the learned linguist, the blind, the deaf and dumb, have but one and the same common way of finding life in it: and he that writes large commentaries upon the Bible, must be saved by something full as different from book-knowledge, as he who can neither write nor read.

For this salvation, which is God's mercy to the fallen soul of man, merely as fallen, must be something that meets every man, and to which every man, as fallen, has something that directs him to turn. For as the fall of man is the reason of this mercy, so the fall must be the guide to it: the want must show the thing that is wanted. And, therefore, the manifestation of this one salvation, or mercy to man, must have a nature suitable, not to this or that great reader of history, or able critic in Hebrew roots and Greek phrases, but suitable to the common state and condition of every son of Adam. It must be something as grounded in the human nature, as the fall itself is; which wants no art to make it known, but to which the common nature of man is the sure and only guide, in one man as well as another. Now this something, which is thus obvious to every man, and which opens the way to Christian redemption in every soul, is "a sense of the vanity and misery of the world; and a prayer of faith and hope to God, to be raised to a better state."

In this sense, to which every man's own nature leads him, lies the whole of man's salvation; here the mercy of God, and the misery of man, are met together; here the fall and the redemption kiss each other. This is the Christianity which is as old as the fall; which alone saved the first man, and can alone save the last. This is it, on which hang all the law and the prophets, and which fulfills them both; for they have only this end, to turn man from the lusts of this life, to a desire, and faith, and hope of a better. Thus does the whole of Christian redemption, considered on the part of man, stand in the same degree of nearness and plainness to all mankind: it is as simple and plain, as the feeling of our own evil and misery; and as natural, as the desire of being saved and delivered from it.

This desire, and faith and hope, of a new life born of God, as our only possible redemption and salvation is the spirit of prayer, that is as opposite to the spirit of this world, as heaven is to hell: the one goes upwards with the same strength as the other goes downwards; the one espouses and unites us to Christ and God, with the same certainty, as the other betroths and weds us to an earthly nature. The spirit of prayer is a pressing forth of the soul out of this earthly life; it is a stretching, with all its desire, after the life of God; it is a leaving as far as it can all its own spirit, to receive a spirit from above to be one life, one love, one Spirit with Christ in God. This prayer, which is an emptying itself of all its own lusts and natural tempers, and an opening itself for the light and love of God to enter into it, is the prayer in "the name of Christ," to which nothing is denied: for the love which God bears to the soul, his eternal, never-ceasing desire to enter into it, to dwell in it, and open the birth of his holy Word and Spirit in it, stays no longer, than till the heart opens to receive him. For "nothing does, or can, keep God out of the soul, or hinder his holy union with it, but the desire of the heart turned from him."

What, therefore, is so necessary for man, as with all his strength to turn from every thing that is not God, and his holy will; and with all the desire, delight, and longing of the heart, to give up himself wholly to the life, light and Spirit of God; pleased with nothing in this world, but as it gives time, and place, and occasions, of doing and being that, which his heavenly Father would have him to do, and be; seeking for no happiness from this earthly, fallen life, but that of overcoming all its spirits and tempers?

To conclude: in the full and true knowledge of the greatness of our fall, and the greatness of our redemption, lie all the reasons of a deep humility, penitences, and self-denial; and also all the motives and incitements to a most hearty, sincere, and total conversion to God: and every one is necessarily more or less a true penitent, and more or less truly converted to God, according as he is more or less deeply or inwardly sensible of these truths. And till these two great truths have both awakened and enlightened our minds, all reformation and pretence to amendment, is but a dead and superficial thing; a mere garment of hypocrisy, to hide us from ourselves and others.

Nothing can truly awaken a sinner, but a true sense of the deep possession and power that sin has in him. When he sees, that sin begins with his being, that it rises up in the essences of his nature, and lives in the first forms of his life; and that he lies thus chained and barred up in the very jaws of death and hell, as unable to alter his own state, as to create another creature; when, with this knowledge, he sees that the free grace of God has provided him a remedy equal to his distress; that he has given him the holy blood and life of Jesus Christ, the true Son of God, to enter as deep into his soul as sin has entered, to change the first forms and essences of his life, and bring forth in them a new birth of a divine nature, that is to be an immortal image of the holy Trinity, everlastingly safe, enriched and blessed, in the bosom of Father, Son, and Holy Ghost; when a man once truly knows and feels these two truths, there seems to be no more that you need do for him. You can tell him of no humility, or pentinenc, or self-abasement, but what is less than his own heart suggests to him: humility can only be feigned or false, before this conviction: he can now no more take any degree of good to himself, than assume any share in the creation of angels; and all pride or self-esteem of any kind, seems to him to contain as great a lie in it, as if he was to say, that he helped to create himself.

You need not tell him, that he must turn unto God with "all his strength, all his heart, all his soul, and all his spirit"—for all that he can offer unto God, seems to him already less than the least of his mercies towards him. He has so seen the exceeding love of God, in the manner and degree of his redemption, that it would be the greatest pain to him, to do any thing but upon a motive of divine love; as his soul has found God to be all love; so it has but one desire, and that is, to be itself all love to God.

This is the conviction and conversion that necessarily arises from a right understanding of these truths; the soul is thereby wholly consecrated to God; and can like, or love, or do nothing but what it can, some way or other, turn into a service of love toward him: but where these truths are not known, or not acknowledged, there it is not to be wondered at, if religion has no root, that is able to bring forth its proper fruits. And if the generality of Christians are a number of dead, superficial consenters to the history of scripture doctrines, as unwilling to have the spirit, as to part with the form of their religion; loth to hear of any kind of self-denial; fond of worldly ease, indulgence and riches; unwilling to be called to the perfection of the gospel; professing and practising religion merely as the fashion and custom of the place they are in requires; if some rest in outward forms, others in a certain orthodoxy of opinions; if some expect to be saved by the goodness of the sect they are of, others by a certain change of their outward behaviour; if some content themselves with a lukewarm spirit, others depend upon their own works; these are delusions that must happen to all who do not know, in some good degree, the true nature of their own fallen soul, and what kind of regeneration alone can save them.

But all these errors, delusions, and false rests, are cut up by the root, as soon as a man knows the true reason and necessity of his wanting so great a Saviour. For he that knows the essences of his soul to be so many essences of sin, which form sin as they form his life; entirely incapable of producing any good, till a birth from God has arisen in them; can neither place his redemption where it is not, nor seek it coolly and negligently where it is.

For knowing that it is the hell within his known nature, that only wants to be destroyed, he is intent only upon bringing destruction upon that; and this secures him from false religion.

And knowing that this inward hell cannot be destroyed, unless God becomes his redeemer or regenerator, in the essences of his soul; this makes him believe all, expect all, and hope all, from his Saviour Jesus Christ alone.

And knowing, that all this redemption, or salvation, is to be brought about in the inmost ground and depth of his heart; this makes him always apply to God, as the God of his heart; and, therefore, what he offers to God, is his own heart; and this keeps him always spiritually alive, wholly employed and intent upon the true work of religion, the fitting and preparing his heart for all the operations of God's holy Spirit upon it. And so he is a true inward Christian, who, as our blessed Lord speaks, has "the kingdom of God within him," where the state and habit of his heart continually and thankfully "worships the Father in spirit and in truth."

—John Payne

BOOK I

Preparatory Instructions
for the Spiritual Life

I

Of the Contempt of
Worldly Vanities

1. "HE that followeth me shall not walk in darkness, but shall
have the light of life." Those are the words of Christ; by which
we are taught, that it is only by a conformity to his life and
spirit, that we can be truly enlightened and delivered from all
blindness of heart: let it, therefore, be the principal employment
of our minds to meditate on the life of Christ.

2. The doctrine of Christ infinitely transcends the doctrine of
the holiest men; and he that had the Spirit of Christ, would find
in it "hidden manna, the bread that came down from heaven:"
but not having his Spirit, many, though they frequently hear his
doctrine, yet feel no pleasure in it, no ardent desire after it; for
he only can cordially receive, and truly delight in the doctrine
of Christ, who continually endeavours to acquire the Spirit, and
imitate the life of Christ.

3. Of what benefit are thy most subtle disquisitions into the mystery of the blessed trinity, if thou art destitute of humility, and, therefore, a profaner of the trinity? It is not profound speculations, but a holy life, that makes a man righteous and good, and dear to God. I had rather feel compunction, than be able to give the most accurate definition of it. If thy memory could retain the whole Bible, and the precepts of all the philosophers, what would it profit thee, without charity and the grace of God? "Vanity of vanities! and all is vanity," except only the love of God, and an entire devotedness to his service.

4. It is the highest wisdom, by the contempt of the world to press forward toward the kingdom of heaven. It is, therefore, vanity to labour for perishing riches, and place our confidence in their possession: it is vanity to hunt after honours, and raise ourselves to an exalted station: it is vanity, to fulfil the lusts of the flesh, and indulge desires that begin and end in torment: it is vanity to wish that life may be long, and to have no concern whether it be good: it is vanity to mind only the present world, and not to look forward to that which is to come; to suffer our affections to hover over a state in which all things pass away with the swiftness of thought, and not raise them to that where true joy abideth for ever.

5. Frequently call to mind the observation of Solomon, that "the eye is not satisfied with seeing, nor the ear filled with hearing;" and let it be thy continual endeavour to withdraw thy heart from the love of "the things that are seen," and to turn it wholly to "the things that are not seen:" for he who lives in subjection to the sensual desires of animal nature, defiles his spirit, and loses the grace of God.

2

Of Humility with Respect to Intellectual Attainments

1. EVERY man naturally desires to increase in knowledge; but what doth knowledge profit, without fear of the Lord? Better is the humble peasant, that serveth God, than the proud philosopher, who, destitute of the knowledge of himself, can describe the course of the planets. He that truly knows himself, becomes vile in his own eyes, and has no delight in the praise of man. If I knew all that the world contains, and had not charity, what would it avail me in the sight of God, who will judge me according to my deeds?

2. Rest from an inordinate desire of knowledge, for it is subject to much perplexity and delusion. Learned men are fond of the notice of the world, and desire to be accounted wise: but there are many things, the knowledge of which has no tendency to promote the recovery of our first divine life; and it is, surely, a proof of folly, to devote ourselves wholly to that, with which

our supreme good has no connexion. The soul is not to be satisfied with the multitude of words; but a holy life is a continual feast, and a pure conscience the foundation of a firm and immoveable confidence in God.

3. The more thou knowest, and the better thou understandest, the more severe will be thy condemnation, unless thy life be proportionably more holy. Be not, therefore, exalted, for any uncommon skill in any art or science; but let the superior knowledge that is given thee, make thee more fearful and more watchful over thyself. If thou supposest, that thou knowest many things, and hast perfect understanding of them, consider, how many more things there are, which thou knowest not at all; and, instead of being exalted with a high opinion of thy great knowledge, be rather abased by an humble sense of thy much greater ignorance. And why dost thou prefer thyself to another, since thou mayest find many who are more learned than thou art, and better instructed in the will of God?

4. If thou would learn and know that which is truly useful, love to be unknown, and to be held in no estimation: for the highest and most profitable learning, is the knowelge and contempt of ourselves, and to have no opinion of our own merit; and always to think well and highly of others, is an evidence of great wisdom and perfection. Therefore, though thou seest another openly offend, or even commit some enormous sin, yet thou must not from thence take occasion to value thyself for thy superior goodness: for thou canst not tell how long thou wilt be able to persevere in the narrow path of virtue. All men are frail, but thou shouldst reckon none so frail as thyself.

3

Of the Knowledge of the Truth

1. BLESSED is the man whom Eternal Truth teacheth, not by obscure figures and transient sounds, but by a direct and full communication! The perceptions of our senses are narrow and dull, and our reasoning on those perceptions frequently misleads us. To what purpose are our keenest disputations on hidden and obscure subjects, for our ignorance of which we shall not be brought into judgment at the great day of universal retribution? How extravagant the folly, to neglect the study of the "one thing needful;" and wholly devote our time and faculties to that, which is not only vainly curious, but sinful and dangerous, as the state of "those that have eyes and see not!"

2. And what have redeemed souls to do with the distinctions and subtleties of logic? He whom the Eternal Word condescendeth to teach, is disengaged at once from the labyrinth of human opinions. For "of one Word are all things;" and all things, without

voice or language, speak him alone: He is that divine principle, which speaketh in our hearts; and without which, there can be neither just apprehension, nor rectitude of judgment. Now he to whom all things are but this one; who comprehendeth, all things in his will, and beholdeth all things in his light, hath "his heart fixed," and abideth in the peace of God.

3. O God, who art the truth, make me one with thee in everlasting love! I am often weary of reading, and weary of hearings in thee alone is the sum of my desires! Let all teachers be silent, let the whole creation be dumb before thee, and do thou only speak unto my soul!

4. The more a man is devoted to internal exercises, and advanced in singleness and simplicity of heart, the more sublime and diffusive will be his knowledge; which he does not acquire by the labour of study, but receives from divine illumination. A spirit pure, simple, and constant, is not, like "Martha, distracted and troubled with the multiplicity of its employments," however great; because, being inwardly at rest, it seeketh not its own glory in what it does, "but doth all to the glory of God;" for there is no other cause of perplexity and disquiet, but an unsubdued will, and unmortified affections. A holy and spiritual man, by reducing them to the rule and standard of his own mind, becomes the master of all his outward acts; he does not suffer himself to be led by them to the indulgence of any inordinate affections that terminate in self, but subjects them to the unalterable judgment of an illuminated and sanctified spirit.

5. No conflict is so severe, as his who labours to subdue himself; but in this we must be continually engaged, if we would be more strengthened in the inner man, and make real progress toward perfection. Indeed, the highest perfection we can attain to in the present state, is alloyed with much imperfection; and our best knowledge is obscured by the shades of ignorance; "we see through a glass darkly:" an humble knowledge of thyself, therefore, is a more certain way of leading thee to God, than the most profound investigations of science. Science, however, or a proper knowledge of the things that belong to the present life, is so far from being blameable, considered in itself, that it is good, and ordained of God; but purity of conscience, and holiness of life, must ever be preferred before it: and because men are more solicitous to learn much, than to live well, they fall into error, and receive little or no benefit from their studies. But if the same diligence was exerted to eradicate vice, and implant virtue, as is applied to the discussion of unprofitable questions, and the "vain strife of words," so much daring wickedness would not be found among the common ranks of men, nor so much licentiousness disgrace those who are eminent for knowledge. Assuredly, in the approaching day of universal judgment, it will not be inquired what we have read, but what we have done; not how eloquently we have spoken, but how holily we have lived.

6. Tell me, where is now the splendour of those learned doctors and professors, whom, while the honours of literature were blooming around them, you so well knew and so highly reverenced? Their prebends and benefices are possessed by others, who scarcely have them in remembrance; the tongue of

fame could speak of no name but theirs while they lived, and now it is utterly silent about them: so suddenly passeth away the glory of human attainments! Had these men been as solicitous to be holy, as they were to be learned, their studies might have been blessed with that honour which cannot be sullied, and that happiness which cannot be interrupted. But many are wholly disappointed in their hopes, both of honour and happiness, by seeking them in the pursuit of "science falsely so called;" and not in the knowledge of themselves, and the love and service of God: and choosing rather to be great in the eyes of men, than meek and lowly in the sight of God, they become vain in their imaginations; and their memorial is written in the dust.

7. He is truly good, who hath great charity: he is truly great, who is little in his own estimation, and rates at nothing the summit of wordly honour: he is truly wise, who "counts all earthly things but as dross, that he may win Christ:" and he is truly learned, who hath learned to abandon his own will, and do the will of God.

4

Of Prudence with Respect to Our Opinions and Actions

1. WE must not believe every word we hear, nor trust the suggestions of every spirit; but consider and examine all things with patient attention, and in reverence to God; for so great, alas! is human frailty, that we are more ready to believe and speak evil of one another, than good. But a holy man is not forward to give credit to the reports of others; because, being sensible of the darkness and malignity of nature, he knows that it is prone to evil, and too apt to pervert truth in the use of speech.

2. It is an evidence of true wisdom, not to be precipitate in our actions, nor pertinacious and inflexible in our opinions; and it is a part of the same wisdom, not to give hasty credit to every word that is spoken, nor immediately to communicate to others what we have heard, or even what we believe. In cases of perplexity and doubt, consult a prudent and religious man; and choose rather to be guided by the counsel of one

better than thyself, than to follow the suggestions of thy own blind will.

3. A holy life, however, makes a man wise according to the divine wisdom, and wonderfully enlargeth his experience: and the more humble his spirit is, and the more subject and resigned to God, the more wise will he become in the conduct of outward life, and the more undisturbed in the possession of himself.

5

Of Reading the Scriptures, and Other Holy Books

1. Not eloquence, but truth, is to be sought after in the Holy Scriptures, every part of which must be read with the same spirit by which it was written. And as in these, and all other books, it is improvement in holiness, not pleasure in the subtlety of the thought, or the accuracy of the exprnssion, that must be principally regarded, we ought to read those parts that are simple and devout, with the same affection and delight, as those of high speculation, or profound erudition.

2. Whatever book thou readest, suffer not thy mind to be influenced by the character of the writer, whether his literary accomplishments be great or small; but let thy only motive to read, be the pure love of truth; and, instead of inquiring who it is that writes, give all thy attention to the nature of what is written. Men pass away like the shadows of the morning; but "the word of the Lord endureth for ever:" and that word,

without respect of persons, in ways infinitely various, speaketh unto all.

3. The profitable reading of the Holy Scriptures, is frequently interrupted by the vain curiosity of our own minds, which prompts us to examine and discuss, and labour to comprehend those parts, that should be meekly and submissively passed over: but to derive spiritual improvement from reading, we must read with humility, simplicity, and faith; and not affect the reputation of profound learning.

4. Ask with freedom, and receive with silence and respect, the instructions of holy men; and let not the parables and allegories of ancient times disgust thee; for they were not written without meaning, and without design.

6

Of Inordinate Affections

1. THE moment a man gives way to inordinate desire, disquietude and torment take possession of his heart. The proud and the covetous are never at rest: but the humble and poor in spirit, possess their souls in the plenitude of peace.

2. He that is not perfectly dead to himself, is soon tempted, and easily subdued, even in the most ordinary occurrences of life. The weak in spirit, who is yet carnal, and inclined to the pleasures of sense, finds great difficulty in withdrawing himself from earthly desires; he feels regret and sorrow, as often as this abstraction is attempted; and every opposition to the indulgence of his ruling passion, kindleth his indignation and resentment. If he succeeds in the gratification of inordinate desire, he is immediately stung with remorse; for he has not only contracted the guilt of sin, but is wholly disappointed of the peace which he sought. It is, therefore, not by indulging, but

by resisting our passions, that true peace of heart is to be found: it cannot be the portion of him that is carnal, nor of him that is devoted to a wordly life; it dwells only with the humble and the spiritual man.

7

Of Vain Hope, and
Elation of Mind

1. HE that placeth his confidence in man, or in any created being, is vain, and trusteth in a shadow. Be not ashamed to serve thy brethren in the meanest offices, and to appear poor in the sight of men, for the love of Jesus Christ. Presume not upon the success of thine own endeavours, but place all thy hope in God: do all that is in thy power with an upright intention, and God will bless with his favour the integrity of thy will. Trust not in thy own wisdom, nor in the wisdom and skill of any human being; but trust in the grace and favour of God, who raiseth the humble, and humbleth the self-presuming.

2. Glory not in riches, though they increase upon thee; nor in thy friends, because they are powerful: but glory in God, who giveth thee riches, and friends, and all things: and, what is more than all, desireth to give thee himself. Be not vain of the gracefulness, strength, and beauty of thy body, which a little sickness

can weaken and deform. Please not thyself with flattering reflections on the acuteness of thy natural wit, and the sweetness of thy natural disposition, lest thou displease God, who is the author of all the good that nature can dispense. Do not think thou art better than others, lest, in the sight of God, who only knoweth what is in man, thou be found worse. Be not proud of that in which thou art supposed to excel, however honoured and esteemed by men; for the judgment of God and the judgment of men are infinitely different; and that displeaseth him which is commonly pleasing to them. Whatever good thou art truly conscious of, think more highly of the good of others, that thou mayest preserve the humility of thy spirit: to place thyself lower than all mankind, can do thee no hurt: but much hurt may be done, by preferring thyself to a single individual. Perpetual peace dwelleth with the humble, but envy, indignation, and wrath, distract the heart of the proud.

8

Of Avoiding the Familiar Intercourses of the World

1. "OPEN not thine heart to every man," but entrust its secrets to him only that is wise, and feareth God. Be seldom in the company of young men and strangers. Flatter not the rich; nor affect to be seen in the presence of the great. Associate only with the humble and simple, the holy and devout; and let thy conversation with them be on subjects that tend to the perfection of thy spirit. Be not familiar with any woman, but recommend all women to the protection and grace of God. Wish to be familiar only with God, and his holy angels, and shun the notice and intimacy of men; charity is due to all, but familiarity is the right of none.

2. It often happens, that a stranger, whom the voice of fame had made illustrious, loses all the brightness of his character, the moment he is seen and known: we hope to please others,

by entering into familiar connexions with them; and we presently disgust them, by the evil qualities, and irregular behaviour, which they discover in us.

9

Of Subjection and Obedience

1. IT is more beneficial to live in subjection, than in authority; and to obey, is much safer than to command. But many live in subjection, more from necessity, than the love of God; and, therefore, pass a life of continual labour, and find occasions of murmur in the most trifling events; nor can they possibly acquire liberty of spirit, until, with the whole heart, they are resigned, in all situations, to the will of God. Go where thou wilt, rest is not to be found, but in humble submission to the divine will: a fond imagination, of being easier in any place than that which Providence has assigned us, and a desire of change grounded upon it, are both deceitful and tormenting.

2. Men love to act from their own judgment, and are always most inclined to those that are of the same opinion with themselves. But if God dwell in our hearts, we shall find it necessary frequently to abandon our own sentiments, for the sake of peace.

And who is so perfectly wise, as to comprehend the causes and connexions of all things? Be not too confident therefore, in thy own judgment, but willingly harken to the judgment of others. And though in a question of speculative knowledge, or a case of worldly prudence, thy own opinion may be good; yet if, for the sake of God, thou canst quietly relinquish it, and submit to the opinion of another, it will greatly conduce to thy spiritual perfection. I have often heard, that it is more safe to take advice, than to give it. In some instances it may happen, that each man's opinion may be so equally good, as to produce suspension on both sides, rather than submission on either; but to refuse submission to the opinion of another, when truth, and the circumstances of the case, require it, is a proof of a proud and pertinacious spirit.

10

Of Superfluous Talking

1. As much as lies in thy power, shun the resorts of worldly men; for much conversation on secular busness, however innocently managed, greatly retards the progress of the spiritual life. We are soon captivated by vain objects and employment, and soon defiled; and I have wished a thousand times, that I had either not been in company, or had been silent.

2. If it be asked, why we are so fond of mixing in the familiar and unprofitable conversations of the world, from which we so seldom return to silence and recollction, without defilement and compunction; it must be answered, because in the present life we seek all our consolation.; and, therefore, hope, by the amusements of company, to efface the impressions of sorrow, and repair the breaches of distraction; and, because of those things that we most love and desire, and of those that we most hate and would avoid, we are fond of thinking and speaking. But, alas!

How deceitful is this artificial management! For the hope of consolation from outward life, utterly destroys that inward and divine consolation which the Holy Spirit gives us, and which is the only support of the soul under all its troubles. Let us, therefore, watch and pray without ceasing, that no part of our invaluable time may be thus sacrificed to vanity and sin; and whenever it is proper and expedient to speak, let us speak those things that are holy, "by which Christians edify one another."

3. An evil habit of negligence and inattention to our growth in grace, is the principal cause of our keeping no guard upon our lips. Spiritual conferences, however, are highly serviceable to spiritual improvement, especially when persons of one heart and one mind associate together in the fear and love of God.

11

Of True Peace of Mind, and
Zeal for Spiritual Improvement

1. WE might enjoy much peace, if we did not busy our minds with what others do and say, in which we have no concern. But how is it possible for that man to dwell long in peace, who continually intermeddles in the affairs of another: who runs abroad seeking occasions of disquietude, and never or but seldom turns to God in the retirement of a recollected spirit? Blessed are the meek and single-hearted, they shall possess the abundance of peace.

2. Whence was it that some of the saints became so perfect in the prayer of contemplation, but because it was their continual study and endeavour to mortify all earthly desires, and abstract themselves from all worldy concerns, that, being free from perturbation, they might adhere to God with all the powers of the soul. But we are too much engaged with our own passions, and too tenderly affected by the business and pleasures of this

transitory life, to be capable of such high attainments: nay, so fixed are our spirits in slothfulness, and cold indifference, that we seldom overcome so much as one evil habit.

3. If we were perfectly dead to ourselves, and free from all inward entanglement, we might then have some relish for divine enjoyments, and begin to experience the blessedness of heavenly contemplation. But the principal if not the only impediment to such a state is, that we continue in subjection to violent passions and inordinate desires, without making the least effort to enter into the narrow way, which Christ has pointed out as the one way of perfection for all the saints of God. Thus, when any adversity, however trifling, comes upon us, we are soon dejected, and have immediate recourse to human consolations: but did we endeavour, like valiant soldiers, to stand our ground in the hour of battle, we should feel the succour of the Lord descending upon us from heaven: for he is always ready to assist those that resolutely strive, and place their whole confidence in the power of his grace; nay, he creates occasions of contest, to bless us with so many opportunities of victory.

4. If the progress to perfection is placed only in external observances, our religion, having no divine life, will quickly perish with the things on which it subsists: but the axe must be laid to the root of the tree, that being separated and freed from the restless desires of nature, and self, we may possess our souls in the peace of God.

5. If every year we did but extirpate one vice, we should soon become perfect men: but we experience the sad reverse of this,

and find that we were more contriet, more pure, more humble, and obedient, in the beginning of our conversion, than after many years' profession of a religious life. It would be but reasonable to expect, that the fervour of our affections, and our progress in holiness, should have advanced higher and higher every day: but it is now thought to be a foundation of comfort, and even of boast, if a man, at the close of this mortal state, is able to retain some degree of his first ardour.

6. That the path of holiness may become easy and delightful, some violence must be used at first setting out, remove its numerous obstructions. It is hard, indeed, to relinquish that to which we have been accustomed; and harder still, to resist and deny our own will. But how can we hope to succeed in the greatest conflict, if we will not contend for victory in the least? Resist, then, thy inordinate desires in their birth; and continually lessen the power of thy evil habits, lest, as they increase in strength, in proportion as they are indulged, they grow at length too mighty to be subdued. O! if thou didst but consider, what peace thou wilt bring to thyself, and what joy thou wilt produce in heaven, by a life conformed to the life of Christ, I think thou wouldest be more watchful and zealous, for thy continual advancement towards spiritual perfection.

12

Of the Benefit of Adversity

1. IT is good for man to suffer the adversity of this earthly life; for it brings him back to the sacred retirement of the heart, where only he finds, that he is an exile from his native home, and ought not to place his trust in any worldly enjoyment. It is good for him also to meet with contradicton and reproach; and to be evil thought of, and evil spoken of, even when his intentions are upright, and his actions blameless; for this keeps him humble, and is a powerful antidote to the poison of vain glory: and then chiefly it is, that we have recourse to the witness within us, which is God, when we are outwardly despised, and held in no degree of esteem and favour among men. Our dependance upon God ought to be so entire and absolute, that we should never think it necessary, in any kind of distress, to have recourse to human consolations.

2. When a regenerate man is sinking under adversity, or disturbed and tempted by evil thoughts, he then feels the necessity

of the power and presence of God in his soul, without which he certainly knows, that he can neither bear evil, nor do good; then he grieves and prays, and "groans to be delivered from the bondage of corruption;" then weary of living in vanity, he wishes to "die," that he may be dissolved, and be with Christ; and then he is fully convinced, that absolute security, and perfect rest, are not compatible with his present state of life.

13

Of Resisting Temptations

1. As long as we continue in this world, we cannot possibly be free from the trouble and anguish of temptation: and in confirmation of this truth, it is written in Job, that "the life of man upon earth is a continual warfare." Every one, therefore, ought to be attentive to the temptations that are peculiar to his own spirit; and to persevere in watchfulness and prayer, lest his "adversary the devil, who never sleepeth, but continually goeth about, seeking whom he may devour," should find some unguarded place, where he may enter with his delusions.

2. The highest degree of holiness, attainable by man, is no security against the assaults of temptation, from which his present life is not capable of absolute exemption. But temptations, however dangerous and afflicting, are highly beneficial; because, under their discipline, we are humbled, purified, and led toward perfection. All the followers of Christ have, through

"much tribulation and affliction, entered into the kingdom of God;" and those that could not endure the trial, have "fallen from the faith and expectation of the saints, and become reprobate."

3. There is no order of men, however holy, nor any place, however secret and remote, where and among whom temptations will not come, for the exercise of meekness, and troubles rise for the trial of patient resignation. And that this must be the condition of human nature in the present life, is evident, because it is born in sin, and contains in itself those restless and inordinate desires, which are the ground of every temptation: so that when one temptation is removed another succeeds; and we shall always have some degree of evil to suffer, till we have recovered the purity and perfection of that state from which we are fallen.

4. Many, by endeavouring to fly from temptations, have fallen precipitately into them; for it is not by flight, but by patience and humility, that we must become superior to all our enemies. He who only declines the outward occasion, and strives not to pluck up the inward principle by the root, is so far from conquest, that the temptation will recur the sooner, and with greater violence, and he will feel the conflict still more severe. It is by gradual advances, rather than impetuous efforts, that victory is obtained; rather by patient suffering that looks up to God for support, than by impatient solicitude, and rigorous austerity.

5. In thine own temptations, often ask counsel of those that have been tried, and have overcome: and in the temptations of thy

brother, treat him not with severity, but tenderly administer the comfort which you desire to receive.

6. That which renders the first assaults of temptation peculiarly severe and dangerous, is the instability of our own minds, arising from the want of faith in God; and as a ship, without a steersman, is driven about by the force of contrary winds, so an unstable man, that has no faith in God, is tossed and borne away upon the wave of every temptation.

7. Gold is tried in the fire, and acceptable men in the furnace of adversity. We frequently know not the strength that is hidden in us, till temptation calls it forth, and shows us how much we are able to sustain. We must not, however, presume; but be particularly upon our guard against the first assaults; for the enemy will be more easily subdued, if he is resisted in his approaches, and not suffered to enter the portal of our hearts.

8. A certain poet gives this advice:

Take physic early; medicines come too late,
When the disease has grown inveterate.

And the caution may be successfully applied to the assaults of sin, the progress of which is gradual and dangerous; for evil is at first presented to the mind by a single suggestion; the imagination, kindled by the idea, seizes it with all its strength, and feeds upon it: this produces sensual delight, then the motions of inordinate desire, and at length the full consent of the will.

And thus, the malignant enemy, that was not resisted in his first attack, enters by gradual advances, and takes entire possession of the heart; and the longer opposition is deferred by habitual negligence, the power of opposing becomes every day less, and the strength of the adversary proportionably greater.

9. To some, temptations are more severe at the beginning of conversion; to others, at the end; some are afflicted with them during the whole course of a religious life; and some experience but short and gentle trials. This variety is adjusted by the wisdom and equity of Divine Providence, which hath weighed the different states and dispositions of different men, and ordered all its dispensations so as most effectually to tend to the salvation of all. Therefore, when we are tempted, let us not despair, but rather, with more animated fervours of faith, hope, and love, pray to God, that he would vouchsafe to support us under all our trials; and, in the language of St. Paul, "with every temptation, to make also a way to escape," that we may be able to bear it; let us humble our souls, as under the hand of God, who hath promised to "save and exalt the lowly and the meek."

10. By these trials of affliction in the spirit of man, his proficiency in the Christian life is fully proved; the power of divine grace is more sensibly felt in himself, and the fruits of it are more illustriously apparent to others. It is, indeed, a little matter, for man to be holy and devout, when he feels not the pressure of any evil: but if, in the midst of troubles, he maintains his faith, his hope, and resignation, and in patience possesses his soul, he gives a considerable evidence of a regenerate nature. Some,

however, who have been blest with victory in combating temptations of the most rigorous kind, are yet suffered to fall even by the lightest, that arise in the occurrences of daily life; that being humbled by the want of power to resist such slight attacks, they may never presume upon their own strength to repel those that are more severe.

14

Of Avoiding Rash Judgment

1. Keep thy eye turned inwardly upon thyself, and beware of judging the actions of others. In judging others a man labours to no purpose, commonly errs, and easily sins; but in examining and judging himself, he is always wisely and usefully employed.

2. We generally judge of persons and things, as they either oppose or gratify our private views and inclinations; and, blinded by the impetuous motions of self-love, are easily led from the judgment of truth. If God alone was the pure object of all our intentions and desires, we should not be troubled when the truth of things happens to be repugnant to our own sentiments and opinions: but now we are continually drawn aside from truth and peace, by some partial inclination lurking within, or some apparent good or evil rising without.

3. Many, indeed, secretly seek themselves in everything they do, and perceive it not. These, while the course of things perfectly coincides with the sentiments and wishes of their own hearts, seem to possess all the blessings of peace; but when their wishes are disappointed, and their sentiments opposed, they are immediately disturbed and become sorrowful and wretched.

4. From the diversity of inclinations and opinions tenaciously adhered to, arise dissentions among friends and countrymen, nay, even among the professors of a religious and holy life.

5. It is difficult to extirpate that which custom has deeply rooted; and no man is willing to be carried further, than his own inclinations and opinions lead him. If, however, thou adherest more to thy own reason, and thy own will, than to the meek obedience of Jesus Christ, as the principle of all virtue within thee, thou wilt but slowly, if ever, receive the illuminations of the Holy Spirit; for God expects an entire and absolute subjection of our will to his; and that the flames of divine love should infinitely transcend the sublimest heights of human reason.

15

Of Works of Charity

1. Let not the hope of any worldly advantage, nor the affection thou bearest to any creature, prevail upon thee to do that which is evil. For the benefit of him, however, who stands in need of relief, a customary good work may sometimes be intermitted, or rather commuted; for, in such a case, that good work is not annihilated, but incorporated with a better.

2. Without charity, the external work profiteth nothing; but whatever is done from charity, however trifling and contemptible in the opinion of men, is wholly fruitful in the acceptance of God, who regardeth more the degree of love with which we act, than what or how much we have performed. He doth much, who loveth much; he doth much, who doth well; and he doth much and well, who constantly preferreth the good of the community, to the gratification of his own will.

3. Many actions, indeed, assume the appearance of charity, that are wholly selfish and carnal; for inordinate affections, self-will, the hope of reward, and the desire of personal advantage and convenience, are the common motives that influence the conduct of men.

4. He that hath true and perfect charity, seeketh not his own in any thing, but seeketh only that "God may be glorified in all things;" he envieth not, for he desires no private gratification: he delighteth not in himself, nor in any created being; but wisheth for that which is infinitely transcendent, to be blest in the enjoyment of God: he ascribes not good to any creature, but refers it absolutely to God, from whom, as from its fountain, all good originally flows; in whom, as in their centre, all saints will finally rest.

5. O that man had but one spark of true charity! He would then know by an experimental feeling, that himself, the world, and all creatures, were altogether vanity.

16

Of Bearing the Infirmities
of Others

1. THOSE evils which a man cannot rectify, either in himself or others, he ought to bear with humble resignation, till God shall be pleased to produce a change; for this state of imbecility is, perhaps, continued as the proper trial of patience, without the perfect work of which we shall make but a slow and ineffectual progress in the Christian life. Yet under these impediments we must devoutly pray, that God would enable us, by the assistance of his Spirit, to bear them with constancy and meekness.

2. If after the first and second admonition, thy brother will not obey the truth, contend no longer with him, but leave the event to God, who only knoweth how to turn evil into good, that his will may be done, and his glory accomplished in all his creatures.

3. Endeavour to be always patient of the faults and imperfections of others; for thou hast many faults and imperfections of thy own, that require a reciprocation of forbearance. If thou art not able to make thyself that which thou wishest to be, how canst thou expect to mould another in conformity to thy will? But we require perfection in the rest of mankind, and take no care to rectify the disorders of our own hearts; we desire that the faults of others should be severely punished, and refuse the gentlest correction ourselves; we are offended at their licentiousness, and yet cannot bear the least opposition to our own immoderate desires; we would subject all to the control of rigorous statutes and penal laws, but will not suffer any restraint upon our own actions; and thus it appears how very seldom the second of the two great commandments of Christ is fulfilled, and how difficult it is for a man to "love his neighbour as he loves himself."

4. If all men were perfect, we should meet with nothing in the conduct of others to suffer for the sake of God. But in the present fallen state of human nature, it is his blessed will, that we should learn to "bear one another's burdens;" and as no man is free from some burden of sin or sorrow; as none has strength and wisdom sufficient for all the purposes of life and duty, the necessity of mutual forbearance, mutual consolation, mutual support, instruction and advice, is founded upon our mutual imperfections, troubles and wants. Besides, by outward occasions of suffering from the conduct of others, the nature and degree of every man's inward strength is more plainly discovered; for outward occasions do not make him frail, but only show him what he is in himself.

17

Of a Recluse Life

1. IT is necessary that thou shouldest learn to break and subdue thy own will, in innumerable instances, if thou wouldest live in harmony and peace among those that are devoted to a life of religious retirement. "How good and how pleasant it is for brethren," in colleges and other societies, separated from the world, "to dwell together in unity, and to preserve the bond of peace unbroken to the end of life! Blessed, surely, is the man, who in this state hath passed his days with innocence, and closed them with success! That thou mayest keep thy integrity, by a faithful perseverance in a course so glorious, consider thyself as an exile from thy native country, a stranger and a pilgrim upon earth, and be willing to become a fool for the sake of Christ.

2. It is not the peculiar habit, the tonsure, or any alteration merely external, but a change of heart, and an entire mortification of the passions, that are the indispensable qualifications

for such a state; and he that seeks any thing in it, but the glory of God, in the purification of his own soul, will meet only with disappointment and trouble, anxiety and remorse; for the blessing of peace cannot long rest upon him who doth not continually endeavour to make himself less than all men, and to become subject to all.

3. But, tell me, for what purpose camest thou hither; to serve or to govern, to be ministered unto, or to minister? Thou knowest, that here thou art called to a life of subjection, labour and patience; not of dominion, idleness and amusement. Here men are tried as gold in the fire; and here no one can stand, unless with his whole heart he desireth to be humbled in the highest degree for the sake of God.

18

Of the Examples of the Holy Fathers

1. CONSIDER the lively examples of the primitive Christians, re-splendent with the heavenly brightness of religious perfection, and you will soon discern how worthless and vain is the sum of our best actions. Alas! what is our life, if it be compared with theirs? Those holy men, the faithful disciples of a crucified Saviour, maintained their allegiance to their Lord, in hunger and thirst, in cold and nakedness, in labour and fatigue, in watching and prayer, in fasting and holy meditation, in the multitude of persecutions and reproaches. How numerous and severe were the trials of the apostles, martyrs, confessors, virgins, and all who desired to "follow Christ in the regeneration!" They "hated their life in this world, that they might keep it unto life eternal."

2. How severe a state of self-renunciation was chosen by the fathers in the desert! What long and heavy temptations did their

perseverance overcome! What reiterated conflicts did they sustain with the enemy! How ardent were their prayers! How rigorous their tasks of abstinence! With what zeal and fervour did they aspire after higher degrees of spiritual perfection! With what intrepidity and resolution did they wage perpetual war against their vices! How pure and disinterested was their love of God! The day they devoted to labour, and the night to prayer; and even in the hours of labour, their heart was lifted up to heaven in continual aspirations. Their whole time was usefully employed; every hour in which they were engaged in immediate intercourse with God, seemed short; and ravished with the surpassing sweetness of divine contemplation, they became insensible of the want of bodily refreshment. Riches, authority, honours, friends, relations, and all propriety in the possession of sublunary good, they renounced; they received, with a reluctant hand, the common supports of animal life, and even deplored the necessity of administering to the wants of the body. With respect, therefore, to all earthly possessions, they were poor; but they were eminently rich in holiness, and the favour of God; outwardly, they were in absolute want; but inwardly, they abounded in grace and the refreshments of divine consolation; they were the aliens and outcasts of the world, but the adopted sons and intimate friends of God; in their own estimation they were less than nothing, and vanity; and were, indeed, mean and despicable in the eyes of men; but in the sight of God, they were elect and precious. By deep humility, pure obedience, ardent charity and persevering patience, they made continual advances in the spiritual life, and obtained superadded degrees of the grace of God. Such were the men that were given for an example to all the professors of a religious life; and though their number is small, yet it ought more to encourage us to press resolutely forward toward perfection, than the multitude of the lukewarm to relax in our endeavours, and linger in our progress.

3. As an effect of the influence of their life, how great was the ardour of religious societies, at their first institution! What devotion in prayer! What emulation in holiness! How strict and impartial the discipline of the superior, how unconstrained and cheerful the reverence and obedience of the subject! These footsteps, though forsaken, still bear testimony to the upright progress of these holy men; who, by persevering in the narrow path in which Christ has called all to follow him, trampled the world under their feet. Now, zeal is contracted within the narrow limits of negative perfection; and a mere passive sufferance of that discipline to which obedience has been vowed, a mere exemption from positive transgression, is esteemed a foundation of triumph. Ah! lamentable supineness! That we should so soon lose the primitive ardour, and grow weary of a life of holiness, through mere idleness and cold indifference.

4. God grant, that in thy heart, which has been impressed with so many examples of true devotion, the desire of perfection may never sleep the sleep of death!

19

Of Religious Exercises

1. THE life of a religious man ought not only so to abound with holiness, as that the frame of his spirit may be at least equal to his outward behaviour; but there ought to be much more holiness within, than is discernible without; because God, who searcheth the heart, is our inspector and judge, whom it is our duty infinitely to reverence, wherever we are, and as angels, to walk pure in his sight. We ought every day to renew our holy resolutions, and excite ourselves to more animated fervour, as if this was the first day of our conversion, and to say—"Assist me, O Lord God, in my resolution to devote myself to thy holy service; and grant, that this day I may begin to walk perfectly, because all that I have done hitherto is nothing."

2. According to the strength of our resolution, so is the degree of our progress; and much diligence and ardour is necessary for him who wisheth to advance well; for if he whose resolutions

are strong, often fails, what will he do, whose resolutions are weak? We break our resolutions, indeed, from various causes, and in various ways; and a slight omission of religious exercises seldom happens without some injury to the spirit.

3. The good resolutions of the righteous depend not upon their own wisdom and ability, but upon the grace of God, in which they perpetually confide, whatever be their attempts; for they know, that "though the heart of man deviseth his way," yet the Lord ordereth the event; and that "it is not in man that walketh, to direct his steps."

4. If, for some act of piety, or some purpose of advantage to thy brother, a customary exercise is sometimes omitted, it may afterward be easily resumed; but if it is lightly relinquished, through carelessness or weariness of spirit, the omission becomes culpable, and will be found hurtful. After the best exertion of our endeavours, we shall still be apt to fail in many duties; some determined resolution, however, must always be made, especially against those tempers and habits that are the chief impediments to our growth in grace.

5. The concerns both of our outward state and inward spirit, are to be equally examined and regulated; because both have a considerable influence in obstructing, or advancing, the spiritual life. If thou canst not continually recollect thyself, do it sometimes at least, and not less than twice every day, in the morning, and in the evening. In the morning, resolve; and, in the evening, examine thy behaviour; what thou hast that day been in thought, word and deed: for in all these, perhaps, thou hast

often offended God and thy brother. Gird thy loins like a valiant man, and be continually watchful against the malicious stratagems of the devil. Bridle the appetite of gluttony, and thou wilt with less difficulty restrain all other inordinate desires of animal nature. Never suffer the invaluable moments of thy life to steal by unimproved, and leave thee in idleness and vacancy; but be always either reading, or writing, or praying, or meditating, or employed in some useful labour for the common good.

6. Bodily exercises are to be used with discretion; and the same exercises must not be indiscriminately undertaken by all. Those to which the duty of the society, as such, does not oblige us, must never be performed in the sight of others; for they are private and personal, and can be safely and usefully performed only in secret. Take care, however, that from the love of private and personal exercises, thou dost not become averse to the public exercises of the community; but having fully and faithfully discharged those to which thou art bound by the injunctions of the superior, if any leisure remains, return to thyself again, and do whatever the spirit of devotion prompts thee to.

7. The same kind of exercise is not equally suited to the state and improvement of every spirit; but some are more useful and convenient to one than to another. Different exercises are also expedient for different times and seasons; and some are more salutary for the days of feasting, and some for the days of fasting; we stand in need of some in the seasons of temptation, and of others in the hours of internal peace and rest; some subjects of meditation are fitter for a time of sorrow, and others when we rejoice in the Lord.

8. On the eve of the principal feasts and fasts, we should renew our holy exercises, and with more exalted fervour implore the mediation of our great Intercessor; and in the intervals between feast and feast, we should form such holy resolutions, as if we were about to leave this earthly life, to be made partakers of the everlasting feast. In all these seasons of peculiar devotion, we ought so to prepare our spirits, and so regulate our actions, as if we were shortly to be admitted into the joy of our Lord. And if that blessed event is still deferred, let us humbly acknowledge, that we are not yet sufficiently prepared for it, but are still unworthy of that great glory which shall be revealed in us, in God's appointed time; and may a contrite sense of such an improper state, quicken us to more faithful vigilance, and a more holy preparation. "Blessed is that servant," saith Christ, "whom his lord, when he cometh, shall find watching. Verily, I say unto you, that he will make him ruler over all that he hath."

20

Of Solitude and Silence

1. Appropriate a convenient part of time to retirement and self-converse, and frequently meditate on the wonderful love of God in the redemption of man. Reject all studies that are merely curious; and read only what will rather penetrate the heart with holy compunction, than exercise the brain with useless speculations.

2. If thou canst refrain from unnecessary conversation and idle visits, and suppress the desire of hearing and telling some new thing, thou wilt find not only abundant leisure, but convenient opportunity, for holy and useful meditation. The most eminent saints, where Providence has permitted it, have shunned all intercourse with men, and chosen to live wholly to God in retirement and solitude.

3. It is the declaration of Seneca, that "as often as he mingled in the company of men, he came out of it less a man than he

went in;" and to the truth of this, our own experience, after much free conversation, bears testimony; for it is much easier to be wholly silent, than not to exceed in word; it is much easier to keep concealed at home, than to preserve ourselves from sin abroad; he, therefore, that presseth forward to the perfection of the internal and spiritual life, must, with Jesus, withdraw himself from the multitude.

4. No man can safely go abroad, that does not love to stay at home; no man can safely speak, that does not willingly hold his tongue; no man can safely govern, that would not cheerfully become subject; no man can safely command, that has not truly learned to obey; and no man can safely rejoice, but he that has the testimony of a good conscience.

5. The joy and safety of the saints has always been full of the fear of God; nor were they less humble, and less watchful over themselves, because of the splendour of their holiness, and their extraordinary measures of grace; but the security of the wicked begins in pride and presumption, and ends in self-delusion. Whatever, therefore, are thy attainments in holiness, do not promise thyself a state of unchangeable perfection in the present life. Those whose character for virtue has stood high in the esteem of men, have been proportionably more exposed to the danger of a severer fall, through self-confidence; and, therefore, it is much safer for most men not to be wholly free from temptation, but rather to be often assaulted, lest they grow too secure; lest, perhaps, they exalt themselves in the pride of human attainments; nay, lest they become wholly devoted to the honours, the pleasures, and comforts of their earthly life.

6. O that man would never seek after transitory joy, would never busy himself with the trifling affairs of a perishing world; how pure a conscience might he maintain! O that he could divorce his spirit from all vain solicitude; and devoting it to the contemplation of God, and the truths of salvation, place all his confidence in the divine mercy; in what profound tranquillity and peace would he possess his soul.

7. No man is worthy of heavenly consolation, unless he hath been diligently exercised in holy compunction. If thou desirest true compunction, enter into thy closet, and, excluding the tumults of the world, according to the advice of the Psalmist, "commune with thy heart and be still," that thou mayest feel regret and horror for sin. Thou wilt find in the closet, that which thou often losest abroad. The closet long continued in, becomes delightful; but, when seldom visited, it is beheld with reluctance, weariness, and disgust. If, in the beginning of thy conversion, thou canst keep close to it, and cultivate the advantages it is capable of yielding, it will be ever after desirable as a beloved friend, and become the seat of true consolation.

8. In solitude and silence the holy soul advances with steady steps, and learns the hidden truths of the oracles of God. There she finds the fountain of tears, in which she bathes and purifies herself every night: there she riseth to a more intimate union with her Creator, in proportion as she leaves the darkness, impurity, and tumult of the world. To him, who withdraws himself from his friends and acquaintance to seek after God, will God draw near with his holy angels.

9. It is better for a man to lie hid continually, and attend to the purification of his soul, than neglecting that one thing needful, to go abroad and work miracles. It is highly commendable in all that are devoted to a religious life, to go seldom abroad, to decline being seen of men, and to be as little fond of seeing them. And indeed, why shouldest thou desire to see that, which thou hast neither power nor permission to enjoy? For the world passeth away, and the lust thereof. Our sensual appetites continually prompt us to range abroad, in search of continual gratification; but when the hour of wandering is over, what do we bring home, but remorse of conscience, and weariness and dissipation of spirit? A joyful going out is often succeeded by a sad return; and a merry evening brings forth a sorrowful morning. Thus all carnal joy enters delightfully, but ere it departs, bites and kills.

10. What canst thou see any where else, which thou canst not see in thy chosen retirement? Behold the heavens, the earth and all the elements! For out of these were all things made. What canst thou see there or any where, that will continue long under the sun? Thou hopest, perhaps, to subdue desire by the power of enjoyment: but thou wilt find it impossible for the eye to be satisfied with seeing, or the ear to be filled with hearing. If all visible nature could pass in review before thee, what would it be but a vain vision?

11. Lift up thy eyes, then, to God in the highest heavens, and pray for the forgiveness of thy innumerable sins and negligences. Leave vain pleasures to the enjoyment of vain men, and mind only that which God hath required of thee for thy own eternal

good. Make thy door fast behind thee; and invite Jesus, thy beloved, to come unto thee, and enlighten thy darkness with his light. Abide faithfully with him in this retirement, for thou canst not find so much peace in any other place.

12. If thou hadst never gone abroad, and listened to idle reports, thou hadst continued safe in the possession of peace. But from whatever time thou delightest to hear and to tell news, thy heart will be the prey of dis appointment and trouble, anxiety and perturbation.

21

Of Compunction of Heart

1. IF thou wouldest make any progress in the Christian life, keep thyself continually in the fear of God; and love not licentious freedom, but restrain all thy senses within strict discipline, and guard thy spirit against intemperate mirth. Give up thy heart to compunction, and thou wilt soon feel enkindled in it the fire of devotion. Compunction opens a path to infinite good, which is instantly lost by dissipation and light merriment. It is wonderful, indeed, that any man should rejoice in this life, who considers his state of banishment, and the multitude of dangers to which he is continually exposed: but through levity of heart, and the neglect of self-examination, we grow insensible of the disorders of our souls; and often vainly laugh when with just reason we ought to mourn. There is, however, no true liberty, nor any solid joy, but in the fear of God, united with a pure conscience.

2. Blessed is the man, who can throw off every impediment of trouble and dissipation, and recollect his spirit into union with holy compunction! Blessed is he, that can renounce every enjoyment that may either defile or burthen his conscience! Strive manfully; one custom is subdued and extirpated by another. If thou canst divorce thyself from men and their concerns, they will soon divorce themselves from thee, and leave thee to do the work of thy own salvation and peace.

3. Perplex not thy spirit, therefore, with the business of others, nor involve thyself in the interests of the great. Keep thy eye continually upon thyself, as its chief object; and admonish thyself, in an especial manner, above all that are dear to thee. Grieve not, that thou dost not enjoy the favour of men; but rather grieve, that thou hast not walked with that holy vigilance and self-denial which becometh a true Christian, who is the devoted servant of God.

4. It is more safe, and more beneficial, not to have many consolations in the present life, especially those that are carnal. That we are destitute, however, of spiritual and divine consolation, or but seldom enjoy its sweetness, is owing to ourselves; because we desire not compunction of heart, nor abandon those consolations that are external and vain. Acknowledge thyself not only unworthy of divine consolation, but worthy rather of much tribulation.

5. When a man feels true compunction, the pleasures and honours of the world become burthensome and bitter, and he finds continual occasion for grief and tears: for whether he considers

himself, or thinks of others, he knows, that no man lives without much tribulation. And the more he considers himself, the greater will be his sorrow: for the ground of true compunction and sorrow, is the multitude of our transgressions, and the strong possession that sin has in us; by which our faculties are so subdued, that we are scarcely ever able to contemplate the enjoyments of the heavenly state.

6. If thou didst more frequently think of the time of death, than of the length of life, thou wouldest undoubtedly exert more ardent resolution in resisting the power of sin: and didst thou truly consider the awful purifications that are necessary to restore a neglected and ill-governed spirit, I think thou wouldest gladly submit to a life of labour and penance, and not be afraid of the most rigorous austerities; but because we suffer not these considerations to impress our hearts, but turn them off by yielding to the blandishments of sense, we remain, both to the evil of our fallen state, and the means of redemption from it, cold and insensible.

7. It is owing to that imbecility which dreads compunction, that the wretched body complains upon such trifling occasions. Pray, therefore, most humbly and most ardently to the Lord, that he would bless thee with the spirit of compunction, and say, with the royal prophet, "Feed me, O Lord, with the bread of tears, and give me plenteousness of tears to drink!"

22

Of the Consideration
of Human Misery

1. WRETCHED thou art, wherever thou art, and to whatever thou turnest, unless thou turnest to God. Why art thou troubled, because the events of life have not corresponded with thy own will and desire? Who is there, that enjoyeth all things according to his own will? Neither I, nor thou, nor any man upon earth. There is no human being, without some share of distress and anguish, not even kings and popes. Whose condition, therefore, is the best? His, surely, who is ready to suffer any affliction for the sake of God.

2. Many weak and ignorant persons say, "Behold, how happy a state does that man enjoy! How rich, how great, how powerful and exalted!" But turn thy attention to the unfading glories, and unperishing riches of eternity, and thou wilt perceive that all these temporal advantages are of no value: their acquisition and continuance are uncertain, and their enjoyment painful; for they

are never possessed without solicitude and fear. The happiness of man, whose real wants are soon and easily supplied, "consisteth not in the abundance of the things which he possesseth."

3. It is, indeed, misery to live upon earth; and the more spiritual a man desires to be, the more bitter does he find the present life; because he more sensibly feels in himself, and more clearly discerns in others, the depths of human corruption. To eat and drink, to wake and sleep, to labour and to rest, and to be subject to all other necessities of fallen nature, must needs be a life of affliction and misery to the regenerate man, who longs "to be dissolved," and to be free from sin, and the occasions of sin.

4. Under a sense of the oppression and trouble which the internal man feels from bodily wants and pains, the royal prophet, so far as it was possible to be freed from them, devoutly prays, "from my necessities deliver me, O Lord!" Miserable, however, are all who have not this sense of the corruption and misery of their present life; and much more miserable those that are in love with it: for there are some whose attachment to it is so exceedingly strong, that though by their own labour, and the bounty of others, they are scarcely supplied with common necessaries, yet if it was possible for them to live here for ages, they would not spend a single thought on the kingdom of God. O infatuated and faithless hearts, that are so deeply sunk in earth, as to feel no desire for any enjoyments but those that are carnal! But, wretched creatures! they will in the end bitterly experience, how vain and worthless that is on which they have set their affections. The saints of God, and all the devoted friends and followers of Christ, regarded not the things that gratified the appetites of the flesh, nor those that

were the objects of popular esteem and pursuit; but their hope and desire panted after the purity and glory of the angelic kingdom: their whole soul was continually elevated to the eternal and invisible enjoyments of heaven, that by the continual influence of what was visible and temporal, it might not be enslaved to the enjoyments of earth.

5. Dear brother! Cast not away the hope of attaining to these spiritual enjoyments: time and opportunity for this are in much mercy still allowed thee: why, then, wilt thou defer thy good purpose from day to day? Arise, this moment, from the deadly sleep of sin, and say, now is the time of action, now is the day of battle, now the season of amendment, "the accepted time, the day of salvation."

6. The hour of distress, is the hour of victory. Thou must pass through fire and water, before thou canst come to refreshment and rest. Unless thou dost violence to thyself, thou wilt never subdue sin. While we carry about us this corruptible body, we cannot be free from the assaults of sin, nor live without weariness and sorrow. We desire, indeed, to be at rest from all misery; but, as; by sin, we lost our innocence, so, with our innocence, we lost our true happiness. It is, therefore, necessary to hold fast our patience, and wait the appointed time, of God's mercy, 'till this iniquity, and the calamities of which it is the cause, "shall be overpast, and mortality be swallowed up of life."

7. How great is human frailty, for ever prone to evil! To day we confess our sins, and to-morrow commit the same sins again: this hour we resolve to be vigilant, and the next act as if we had

never resolved at all. What reason, therefore, have such corrupt and unstable creatures to be continually humble, and to reject every vain opinion of their own strength and goodness!

8. That may be soon lost through negligence, which after much labour we have at length scarcely attained through grace: and what will become of us in the eve of life, if we grow cool and languid in the morning? Woe be to us, if we thus turn aside to repose and ease, as if all were peace and security; when as yet there does not appear a single footstep of true holiness in all our conduct!

9. We have still need, like young noviciates, of being again instructed; and, by severe dicipline, formed a second time to holiness; if peradventure any hope be left of future amendment, and a more sure advancement toward the perfection of the spiritual life.

23

Of the Meditation of Death

1. The end of thy present life will speedily come: consider, therefore, in what degree of preparation thou standest for that which will succeed. To-day man is, to-morrow he is not seen; and when he is once removed from the sight of others, he soon passeth from their remembrance. O the hardness and insensibility of the human heart, that thinks only on present enjoyments, and wholly disregards the prospects of futurity! In every thought, and every action, thou shouldest govern and possess thy spirit so absolutely, as if thou wast to die to-day; and was thy conscience pure, thou wouldest not fear thy dissolution, however near. It is better to avoid sin, than to shun death. If thou art not prepared for that awful event to-day, how wilt thou be prepared to-morrow? To-morrow is an uncertain day; and how knowest thou, that to-morrow will be thine?

2. What availeth it to live long, when the improvement of life is so inconsiderable? Length of days, instead of making us better, often increaseth the weight of sin. Would to God that we could live well, only for one day! Many reckon years from the time of their conversion; but the account of their attainments in holiness, is exceedingly small. Therefore, though death be terrible, yet a longer life may be dangerous. Blessed is the man, who continually anticipates the hour of his death, and keeps himself in continual preparation for its approach!

3. If thou hast ever seen another die, let not the impression of that most interesting sight be effaced from thy heart; but re-member, that through the same vale of darkness thou also must pass from this state of existence to the next. When it is morn-ing, think that thou mayest not live till the evening; and in the evening presume not to promise thyself another morning. Be, therefore, always ready; and so live, that death may not find thee confounded at its summons. Many die suddenly and un-expectedly; for in such an hour as ye think not, the son of man cometh. And when that last hour is come to thee, thou wilt begin to think differently of thy past life, and be inexpressibly grieved for thy remissness and inconsideration.

4. How wise and happy is the man, who continually endeavours to be as holy in the day of life, as he wishes to be found in the hour of death! And a perfect contempt of the world, an ardent desire of improvement in holiness, the love of discipline, the labour of penitence, cheerful obedience, self-denial, and the

patient enduring of any affliction for the sake of Christ will contribute to raise a pleasing confidence of dying well.

5. While thy mind is invigorated by the health of thy body, thou wilt be able to do much toward thy purification; but when it is oppressed and debilitated by sickness, I know not what thou canst do. Few spirits are made better by the pain and langour of sickness; as few great pilgrims become eminent saints.

6. Let not the example of thy friends and relations, nor any confidence in the superiority of their wisdom, influence thee to defer the care of thy salvation to a future time; for all men, even thy friends, and relations, will forget thee much sooner than thou supposest. It is better to provide oil for thy lamp now, before it is wanted, than to depend upon receiving it from others, "when the bridegroom cometh:" for if thou art not careful of thyself now, who can be careful of thee hereafter, when time and opportunity are for ever lost? This instant, NOW, is exceedingly precious; now is "the accepted time, now is the day of salvation." How deplorable, therefore, is it, not to improve this invaluable moment, in which we may lay hold on eternal life? A time will come, when thou shalt wish for one day, nay, one hour, to repent in; and who can tell, whether thou wilt be able to obtain it?

7. Awake then, dearest brother, and behold from what inconceivable danger thou mayest now deliver thyself; from what horrible fear thou mayest now be rescued, only by "passing the time of thy sojourning in holy fear," and in continual expectation of thy removal by death. Endeavour now to live in such a manner, that, in that awful moment, thou mayest rejoice rather

than fear. Learn now to die to the world, that thou mayest then begin to live with Christ: learn now to despise all created things, that being delivered from every incumbrance, thou mayest then freely rise to him. Now subdue thy earthly and corruptible body, by penitence and self-denial, that then thou mayest enjoy the glorious hope of exchanging it for a spiritual and immortal body, in the resurrection of the just.

8. Ah, foolish man! Why dost thou still flatter thyself with the expectation of a long life, when thou canst not be secure of a single day? How many unhappy souls, deluded by this hope, are in some unexpected moment separated from the body! How often dost thou hear, that one is slain, another is drowned, another by falling from a precipice has broken his neck, another is choked in eating, another has dropped down dead in the exercise of some favorite diversion; and that thousands, indeed, are daily perishing by fire, by sword, by the plague, or by the violence of robbers! Thus is death common to every age; and man suddenly passeth away as a vision of the night.

9. Who will remember thee after death, who will then pray for thee? And whose prayer can then avail thee? Now, therefore, dearest brother, now turn to God, and do whatever his Holy Spirit enables thee to perform; for thou knowest not the hour in which death will seize thee, nor canst thou conceive the consequences of his seizing thee unprepared. Now, while the time of gathering riches is in much mercy continued, lay up for thyself the substantial and unperishing treasures of heaven. Think of nothing, but the business of thy redemption; be careful for nothing, but the improvement of thy state in God. Now "make to thyself friends" of

the regenerated and glorified sons of God, that when thy present life "shall fail, they may receive thee into everlasting habitations.

10. Live in the world as a stranger and pilgrim, who hath no concern with its business or pleasures: and knowing that thou hast "here no continuing city," keep thy heart disengaged from earthly passions and pursuits, and lifted up to heaven in the patient "hope of a city that is to come, whose builder and maker is God." Thither let thy daily prayers, thy sighs, and tears, be directed; that after death thy spirit may be wafted to the Lord, and united to him for ever. Amen.

24

Of the Last Judgment, and the Punishment of Sinners

1. In all thy thoughts and desires, thy actions and pursuits, "have respect to the end;" and consider how thou wilt appear before that awful judge, from whom nothing is hidden, who is not to be perverted by bribes, nor softened by excuses, but invariably judgeth righteous judgment. O most wretched and foolish sinner, thou who tremblest before the face of an angry man, that is ignorant in all things! what wilt thou be able to answer unto God, who knoweth all thy sins, and searchest the lowest depths of the evil that is in thee? Why lookest thou not forward, and preparest thyself for the day of his righteous judgments, in which one man cannot possibly be excused or defended by another, but every one will have as much as he can answer, in answering for himself?

2. The patient man hath, in this world, a true and salubrious purification; who, when he is injured, is more grieved for the

sin of the offender, than for the wrong that is done to himself: who can ardently pray for his enemies, and from his heart forgive their offences; who feels no reluctance to ask forgiveness of others; who is sooner moved to compassion, than provoked to anger: who constantly denies his own will, and endeavours to bring the body into absolute and total subjection to the spirit. And it is, surely, better to purge away sin by continual repentance, and to break off evil habits by continual resistance, in the present life. But through an inordinate love for the indulgences of corrupt flesh and blood, we deceive ourselves into total ignorance and negligence, with respect to all the interests of our immortal spirits.

3. As thy soul is unperishable, what can the fire of purgatory devour but thy sins? The more, therefore, thou now indulgest thyself, and gratifies the desires of thy flesh, the more severe must be thy future suffering, and the more fuel dost thou heap up as food for that fire. The pains of that tremendous state will arise from the nature and degree of every man's sins. There the spiritual sluggard shall be incessantly urged with burning stings, and the glutton tortured with inconceivable hunger and thirst; there the luxurious and voluptuous shall be overwhelmed with waves of flaming pitch and offensive sulphur; and the envious, with the pain of disappointed malignity, shall howl like mad dogs: the proud shall be filled with shame, and the covetous straitened in inexpressible want. One hour of torment there, will be more insupportable, than an hundred years of the severest penance in this life: there, no respite of pain, no consolation of sorrow, can be found; while here, some intermission of labour, some comfort from holy friends, is not incompatible with the most rigorous discipline.

4. Be now, therefore solicitous for thy redemption, and afflicted for the sins that oppose it, that in the day of judgment thou mayest stand securely among the blessed; for "then shall the righteous man stand in great boldness before the face of such as have afflicted and oppressed him." Then shall he rise up in judgment, who now meckly submits to the judgment of others; then the humble and poor in spirit shall have great confidence, and the proud shall be encompassed with fear on every side: then it will be evident to all, that he was wise in this world, who had learned to be despised as a fool for the love of Christ: then the remembrance of tribulation patiently endured will become sweet, and all iniquity shall stop her mouth: then every devout man shall rejoice, and every impious man shall mourn: then shall the mortified and subdued flesh triumph over that which was pampered in ease and indulgence: the coarse garment shall shine, and the soft raiment lose all its lusire; and the homely cottage shall be more extolled than the gilded palace; then constant patience shall give that stability, which the power of the world could not confer; then simple obedience shall be more highly prized than refined subtlety, and a pure conscience more than learned philosophy; then the contempt of riches shall be of more value than all the treasures of worldly men; then shalt thou have greater comfort from having prayed devoutly every day, than from having fared deliciously; and shalt more rejoice, that thou hast kept silence long, than that thou hadst talked much; then works of holiness shall avail thee more than the multitude of fine words; then a life of self-denial shall give thee more satisfaction than all earthly delights could bestow.

5. Learn, therefore, now to suffer under afflictions comparatively light, that thou mayest then be delivered from sufferings

so grievous. Here thou mayest first make trial, how much there thou wilt be able to sustain; for if thou art able to bear but little now, how wilt thou then bear such amazing and lasting torments? If only a slight suffering makes thee so impatient now, what will the rage of hell do then? Behold and consider! Thou canst not have a double paradise; thou canst not enjoy a life of delight and pleasure upon earth, and afterward reign with Christ in heaven.

6. If to this very day thou hadst lived in honour and pleasure, what would it avail, if thou art to die the next moment? All therefore, is vanity, but the love of God, and a life devoted to his will. He that loveth God with all his heart, fears neither death, nor punishment, nor judgment, nor hell; because "perfect love casteth out fear," and openeth a sure and immediate access to the divine presence. But it is no wonder, that he, who still loves and delights in sin, should fear both death and judgment. Yet, however, it might be well, if thou art not to be withheld from sin by the love of God, that thou shouldst at least be restrained from it by fear; for he that casts behind him the fear of an offended God, cannot possibly persevere in anything that is good, but must run precipitately into every snare of the devil.

25

Of Zeal in the Total Reformation of Life

1. BE watchful and diligent in the service of God: and frequently recollect, that thou hast left the broad way of the world, and entered into the narrow path of holiness, that thou mightest live to God, and become a spiritual man. With increasing ardour, therefore, press continually toward the mark, and ere long thou wilt receive the prize of the high calling of God in Christ Jesus: when there shall he no more fear nor sorrow, for God shall wipe all tears from our eyes, and take away all trouble from our hearts. Thus will a short life of inconsiderable labour be exchanged for an everlasting life, not only of perfect rest, but of increasing joy. If thou continuest faithful and diligent in labouring, God doubtless will be faithful and rich in recompensing. Thou mayest, therefore, maintain a comfortable hope, that in the end thou shalt inherit the crown of victory; only beware of security, lest it betray thee into sloth or presumption.

2. A certain person, deeply perplexed about the state of his soul, and continually fluctuating between hope and fear, came one day to a church, overwhelmed with grief, and prostrating himself before the altar, repeatedly uttered this wish in his heart: "O that I certainly knew that I should be able to persevere!" Immediately the divine voice speaking within him, answered thus: "And what wouldst thou do, if this certain knowledge was bestowed upon thee? Do now, that which thou wouldst then do, and rest secure of thy perseverance." Comforted and established by this answer, he resigned himself to the divine disposal, and his perplexity and distress were soon removed. Instead of indulging anxious inquiries into the future condition of his soul, he applied himself wholly to know what was the good and acceptable will of God, as the only principle and perfection of every good work. "Trust in the Lord, and do good," saith the royal prophet; "so shalt thou dwell in the land, and be fed with the riches of his grace."

3. The principal obstacle to the reformation and improvement of life, is the dread of the difficulty, and labour of the contest. And it is true, that they only make the most eminent advance in holiness, who resolutely endeavour to conquer in those things that are most disagreeable and most opposite to their appetites and desires; and then chiefly does a man most advance, and obtain higher degrees of the grace of God, when he most overcomes himself, and most mortifies his own spirit.

4. But though all men have not the same degree of evil to overcome, yet a diligent Christian, zealous of good works, who has more and stronger passions to subdue, will be able to make a

greater progress, than he that is inwardly calm, and outwardly regular, but less fervent in the pursuit of holiness.

5. Two things are highly useful to perfect amendment: to withdraw from those sinful gratifications to which nature is most inclined, and to labour after that virtue in which we are most deficient. Be particularly careful also to avoid chiefly those tempers and actions, that chiefly and most frequently displease thee in others. Wherever thou art, turn everything to an occasion of improvement; if thou beholdest or hearest of good examples, let them kindle in thee an ardent desire of imitation; if thou seest anything blameable, beware of doing it thyself; or if thou hast done it, endeavour to amend it the sooner. As thy eye observeth, and thy judgment censureth others, so art thou observed and censured by them.

6. If it is good and pleasant to behold brethren in the same religious society, full of fervour and devotion in spirit, modest, courteous, and submissive, in their outward deportment; it must be proportionably grievous and offensive, to find among them a dissolute and inordinate life, totally repugnant to the obligations of that holy state which all have freely chosen. How dangerous and hurtful is it, to forget the nature and design of so great a salvation, and turn all the thoughts and desires of the heart to that which is not only foreign to it, but its greatest enemy, a sensual and worldly life.

7. Be mindful, therefore, of that holy vocation with which thou hast been called, and keep continually impressed upon thy mind the image of the crucified Jesus. Thou wilt find abundant reason

to be ashamed and confounded, when, after considering the life of Christ, thou reviewest thy own, which, though thou hast long professed the imitation of that blessed Exemplar, thou hast yet taken so little care to make conformable to it. He that intently and devoutly exercises himself in the most holy life and passion of his Lord, will find all that is useful and necessary to his redemption in such great abundance, that he need not seek after anything out of or better than Jesus. O, if Jesus crucified would come into our hearts, how soon and how sufficiently would we be taught!

8. The zealous and watchful Christian bears patiently, and performs cheerfully, whatever is commanded him: but he that is cold and negligent, suffers tribulation upon tribulation, and of all men is most miserable; for he is destitute of inward and spiritual comfort, and to that which is outward and carnal, he is forbidden to have recourse. He that obstinately throws off the restraints of Christ's easy yoke, is not only in danger of irrecoverable ruin, but will find himself deceived in the expectation of a life of relaxation and liberty; for restraint, opposition, and disgust, will perpetually arise, wherever he turns the imaginations and desires of his heart.

9. But do thou consider the example of those who have voluntarily submitted to the severest discipline; who live in a state of total abstraction from the pleasures and cares of animal life; who go abroad seldom, eat sparingly, clothe coarsely, labour much, talk little, watch late, rise early, pray long, read often, and always keep their spirits under the restraint of some holy exercise. Consider also the spiritual and divine life of the apos-

tles and first followers of Christ, as the object of thy imitation; and doubt not but the mercy of God to all that turn the desire of their heart to him, will enable thee to follow it. In this path thou mayest go forward with increasing hope and strength; and, in this path, thou wilt approach heaven with such speedy steps, as soon to despise and forget all human strength, consolation, and dependance.

10. Would to God that we had no other employment, but with heart and voice to glorify his holy name! That we never stood in need of meat, drink, or sleep, but could always praise God, and attend to the illuminating and purifying influences of his Holy Spirit! The blessedness of the divine life would not then be interrupted, as it is now, by the numerous infirmities and necessities of the body. O that these necessities were wholly removed; and we had nothing to hunger after, but those spiritual refreshments which we now so seldom taste.

11. When a man is so far advanced in the Christian life, as not to seek consolation from any created thing, then doth he first begin perfectly to enjoy God; then, in whatever state he is, he will therewith be content; then, neither doth prosperity exalt, nor adversity depress him; but his heart is wholly fixed and established in God, who is his all in all; with respect to whom, nothing perisheth, nothing dieth; but all things live to his glory, and are continually subservient to his blessed will.

12. Be always mindful of the great end of temporary nature; and remember, that time once lost will never return. Without perpetual watchfulness and diligence, holiness can never be attained;

for the moment thou beginnest to relax in these, thou wilt feel inward imbecility, disorder, and disquietude. But if thou press forward, with unabated fervour, thou shalt find strength and peace; and through the mercy of God, and that love of holiness which his grace hath inspired, wilt perceive thy yoke become daily more easy, and thy burthen more light. Reflect, that it is only the fervent and diligent soul that is prepared for all duty, and for all events; that it is greater toil to resist evil habits, and violent passions, than to sweat at the hardest bodily labour; that he who is not careful to resist and subdue small sins, will insensibly fall into greater; and that thou shalt always have joy in the evening, if thou hast spent the day well. Watch over thyself, therefore; excite and admonish thyself; and, whatever is done by others, do not neglect thyself. Thou wilt make greater advances in imitating the life of Christ, in proportion to the greater violence with which thou deniest thyself. Amen.

BOOK II

Instructions for
the More Intimate Enjoyment
of the Spiritual Life

1

Of Internal Conversation

1. "THE kingdom of God is within you," saith our blessed Redeemer. Abandon, therefore, the cares and pleasures of this wretched world, and turn to the Lord with all thy heart, and thy soul shall find rest. If thou withdrawest thy attention from outward things, and keepest it fixed upon what passeth within thee, thou wilt soon perceive the "coming of the kingdom of God;" for the "kingdom of God" is that "peace and joy in the Holy Ghost," which cannot be received by sensual and worldly men. Christ will come to thee and bless thee with the splendour of his presence, if thou preparest within thee an abode fit to receive him: all his glory and beauty are manifested within, and there he delights to dwell; his visits there are frequent, his condescension amazing, his conversation sweet, his comforts refreshing, and the peace that he brings passeth all understanding.

2. O faithful soul, dispose thy heart for the reception of this bridegroom, who will not fail to fulfil the promise which he hath made thee in these words: "If a man love me, he will keep my words: and my Father will love him; and we will come unto him, and make our abode with him." Give, therefore, free admission to Christ, and exclude all others as intruders. When thou possessest Christ, thou art rich, and canst want no other treasure: he will protect thee so powerfully, and provide for thee so liberally, that thou wilt not any more have need to depend upon the caprice of men. Men are changeable and evanescent as "the morning cloud;" but Christ abideth eternally, and in him thy fountain of strength and peace will flow for ever.

3. Thou must not place any confidence in frail and mortal men, however endeared by reciprocal affection or offices of kindness: nor art thou to be grieved, when, from some change in their temper, they become unfriendly and injurious; for men are inconstant as the wind, and he that is for thee to-day, may to-morrow be against thee. But place thy whole confidence in God, and let him be all thy fear, and all thy love; he will answer for thee against the great accuser, and do that which is most conducive to thy deliverance from evil.

4. Here thou hast "no continuing city;" and whatever be thy situation, thou art "a stranger and a pilgrim," and canst never obtain rest, till thou art united to Christ. Why then dost thou stand gazing about the earth, when the earth is not the seat of thy repose? Thy dwelling-place is in heaven; and earthly objects are only to be transiently viewed, as thou returnest to it; they are all hurried away in the resistless current of time, and thy

earthly life together with them; beware, therefore, of adhering to them, lest thou be bound captive in their chains, and perish in their ruin. Let thy thoughts dwell with the Most High, and thy desire and prayer ascend without intermission to Christ.

5. When thou art not able to contemplate the high mysteries of redemption, and the wonders of the glorified state, think on the passion on the passion of Christ, and let thy soul dwell securely in his most holy wounds: for if, in the severest tribulation, thou canst devoutly fly for refuge to the wounds and stripes of Jesus, thou wilt find abundant strength and comfort, and wilt be so far from being disturbed by the contempt of pride, that thou wilt bear with meekness and tranquillity the most envenomed shafts of calumny.

6. Christ was rejected of men; and, in the extremity of distress, forsaken by his disciples and friends. Christ chose to suffer thus, and to be thus deserted and despised; and dost thou complain of injury and contempt from others? Christ had enemies and slanderers; and wilt thou have all men to be thy friends and admirers? How can thy patience be crowned in heaven, if thou wilt have no adversity to struggle with on earth? Canst thou be the friend and follower of Christ, and not the partaker of his sufferings? Thou must, therefore, suffer with Christ, and for his sake, if thou indeed desirest to reign with him.

7. If thou hadst but once known the fellowship of "the sufferings of Jesus," and been sensible, though in a small degree, of the divine ardour of his love, thou wouldst be wholly indifferent about thy own personal share in the good and evil of the

present life; and far from courting the favour and applause of men, wouldst rather rejoice to meet with their reproach and scorn; for the love of Jesus hath the peculiar virtue of making the soul in which it dwells utterly despise itself. He that loves Jesus, who is the Truth, as the Saviour within him, and is delivered from the slavery of inordinate desire, can always freely turn to God, and, raising himself in spirit above himself, enjoy some portion of the blessed repose of heaven.

8. That man is truly wise, and taught not of men but of God, who perceiveth and judgeth of things as they are in themselves, and not as they are distinguished by names and general estimation. He that has known the power of the spiritual life, and withdrawn his attention from the perishing interests of the world, requires neither time nor place for the exercise of devotion: he can soon recollect himself, because he is never wholly engaged by sensible objects; his tranquillity is not interrupted by bodily labour or inevitable business, but with calmness and composure he accommodates himself to all events as they take place; he is not moved by the capricious humours and perverse behaviour of men; and his constant experience has convinced him, that the soul is no further obstructed and disturbed in its progress towards perfection, than as it is under the power and influence of the present life.

9. If the frame of thy spirit was in right order, and thou wert inwardly pure, all outward things would conduce to thy improvement in holiness, and work together for thy everlasting good: and because thou art now disgusted by a thousand objects, and disturbed by a thousand events, it is evident that thou art not yet "crucified to the world, nor the world to thee."

10. Nothing entangles and defiles the heart of man so much, as the inordinate and impure love of the creatures: but if thou canst abandon the hope of consolation in the enjoyments of earthly and sensual life, thou wilt soon be able to contemplate the glory and blessedness of the heavenly state; and wilt frequently partake of that spiritual consolation which the world can neither give nor take away.

2

Of Humble Submission to Reproof and Shame

1. REGARD not much what man is for thee, nor what against thee; but let it be thy principal care and concern, that God may be with thee in every purpose and action of thy life. Keep thy conscience pure, and God will be thy continual defence; and him whom God defends, the malice of man hath no power to hurt. If thou hast learned to suffer in silent and persevering patience, thou shalt certainly see the salvation of the Lord: he knoweth the properest season of thy deliverance, and will administer the most effectual means to accomplish it; and to his blessed will thou shouldst always be perfectly resigned. It is the prerogative of God, to give help under every trouble, and deliverance from all dishonour.

2. It is useful for preserving the humility of our spirit, that other men should know and reprove our manifold transgressions: and in cases of injury among brethren, the more humble the ac-

knowledgment of the offence is, the more effectually will the offended person be appeased and reconciled.

3. The humble man God protects and delivers; the humble he loves and comforts; to the humble he condescends; on the humble he bestows more abundant measures of his grace, and after his humiliation exalts him to glory; to the humble he reveals the mysteries of redemption, and sweetly invites and powerfully draws him to himself. The humble man, though surrounded with the scorn and reproach of the world, is still in peace; for the stability of his peace resteth not upon the world, but upon God.

4. Do not think that thou hast made any progress toward perfection, till thou feelest that thou art less than the least of all human beings.*

---

* As a demand so mortifying to the pride of human virtue, will be more generally ascribed to the influence of the malignant gloom of a cloister, than to the dictates of the Spirit of Truth, I have selected the following passage from "The Rev. Mr. Law's Serious Call to a Devout and Holy Life;" in which the obligations to the humility here required, are considered upon right principles, and determined with a power of demonstration peculiar to the writings of that excellent divine.

"After this general consideration of the guilt of sin, which has done so much mischief to your nature, and exposed it to so great punishment; and made it so odious to God, that nothing less than so great an atonement of the Son of God, and so great repentance of our own, can restore us to the divine favour.

"Consider next your own particular share in the guilt of sin. And if you would knew with what zeal you ought to repent yourself, consider how you would exhort another sinner to repentance; and what repentance and amendment you would expect from him, whom you judged to be the greatest sinner in the world.

"Now this case every man may justly reckon to be his own. And you may fairly look upon yourself to be the greatest sinner that you know in the world.

"For though you may know abundance of people to be guilty of some gross sins, with which you cannot charge yourself; yet you may justly condemn yourself, as the greatest sinner that you know. And that for these following reasons:

"First, Because you know more of the folly of your own heart, than you do of other people's; and can charge yourself with various sins that you only know of yourself, and cannot be sure that other sinners are guilty of them. So that as you know more of the folly, the baseness, the pride, the deceitfulness and negligence of your own heart, than you do of any one's else, so you have just reason to consider yourself as the greatest sinner that you know; because you know more of the greatness of your own sins, than you do of other people's.

"Secondly, The greatness of our guilt arises chiefly from the greatness of God's goodness towards us; from the particular graces, and blessings, the favours, the lights and instructions that we have received from him.

"Now as these graces and blessings, and the multitude of God's favours towards us, are the great aggravations of our sins against God, so they are only known to ourselves. And, therefore, every sinner knows more of the aggravations of his own guilt, than he does of other people's; and consequently may justly look upon himself to be the greatest sinner that he knows.

"How good God has been to other sinners, what light and instruction he has vouchsafed to them, what blessings and graces they have received from him, how often he has touched their hearts with holy inspirations, you cannot tell. But all this you know of yourself; therefore you know greater aggravations of your own guilt, and are able to charge yourself with greater ingratitude than you can charge upon other people.

"And this is the reason, why the greatest saints have in all ages condemned themselves as the greatest sinners; because they knew some aggravations of their own sins, which they could not know of other people's.

"The right way, therefore, to fill your heart with true contrition, and a deep sense of your own sins, is this: You are not to consider or compare the outward form, or course of your life, with that of other people's; and then think yourself to be less sinful than they, because the outward course of your life is less sinful than theirs.

"But, in order to know your own guilt, you must consider your own particular circumstances; your health, your sickness, your youth or age, your particular calling, the happiness of your education, the degrees of light and instruction that you have received, the good men that you have conversed with, the admonitions that you have had, the good books that you have read, the numberless multitude of divine blessings, graces, and favours that you have received, the good motions of grace that you have resisted, the resolutions of amendment that you have often broken, and the checks of conscience that you have disregarded.

"For it is from these circumstances, that every one is to state the measure and greatness of his own guilt. And as you know only these circumstances of your own sins, so you must necessarily know how to charge yourself with higher degrees of guilt, than you can charge upon other people. God Almighty knows greater sinners, it may be, than you are; because he sees and knows the circumstances of all men's sins; but your own heart, if it is faithful to you, can discover no guilt so great as your own; because it can only see in you those circumstances, on which great part of the guilt of sin is founded.

"You may see sins in other people, that you cannot charge upon yourself; but then you know a number of circumstances of your own guilt, that you cannot lay to their charge.

"And, perhaps, that person that appears at such a distance from your virtue, and so odius in your eyes, would have been much better than you are, had he been altogether in your circumstances, and received all the same favours and graces from God that you have.

"This is a very humbling reflection, and very proper for those people to make, who measure their virtue, by comparing the outward course of their lives with that of other people's. For look at whom you will, however different from you in his way of life, yet you can never know that he has resisted so much divine grace as you have; or that, in all your circumstances, he would not have been much truer to his duty than you are.

"Now this is the reason why I desired you to consider, how you would exhort that man to confess and bewail his sins, whom you looked upon to be one of the greatest sinners. Because if you will deal justly, you must fix the charge at home, and look no farther than yourself. For God has given no one any power of knowing the true greatness of any sins, but his own: and, therefore, the greatest sinner that every one knows, is himself.

"You may easily see how such an one, in the outward course of his life, breaks the laws of God; but then you can never say, that had you been exactly in all his circumstances, you should not have broken them more than he has done.

"A serious and frequent reflection upon these things, will mightily tend to humble us in our own eyes, make us very apprehensive of the greatness of our own guilt, and very tender in censuring and condemning other people. For who would dare to be severe against other people, when for ought he can tell, the severity of God may be more due to him, than to them? Who would exclaim against the guilt of others, when he considers, that he knows more of the greatness of his own guilt, than he does of theirs?

"How often you have resisted God's Holy Spirit; how many motives to goodness you have disregarded; how many particular blessings you have sinned against; how many good resolutions you have broken; how many checks and admonitions of conscience you have stifled, you very well know: But how often this has been the case of other sinners, you know not. And, therefore, the greatest sinner that you know, must be yourself.

"Whenever, therefore, you are angry at sin or sinners, whenever you read or think of God's indignation and wrath at wicked men; let this teach you to be the most severe in your censure, and most humble and contrite in the acknowledgment and confession of your own sins; because you know of no sinner equal to yourself!"

* Law's Serious Call to a Devout and Holy Life

3

Of Peacefulness

1. THOU must first secure the peace of thy own breast, before thou wilt be qualified to restore peace to others. Peacefulness is a more useful acquisition than learning. The wrathful and turbulent man, who is always ready to impute wrong, turneth even good into evil; the peaceful man turneth all things into good. He that is established in peace, is exempt from suspicion; but he that is discontented and proud, is tormented with jealousy of every kind; he has no rest himself, and be will not allow rest to others; he speaketh what he ought to suppress, and suppresseth what he ought to speak; he is watchful in observing the duty of others, and totally negligent with respect to his own. But let thy zeal be exercised in thy own reformation, before it attemps the reformation of thy neighbour.

2. Thou art very skilful and ingenious in palliating and excusing thy own evil actions, but canst not frame an apology for the actions

of others, nor admit it when it is offered by themselves. It would, however, be more just, always to excuse thy brother, and accuse thyself. If thou desirest to be borne with, thou must bear also with others. O consider, at what a dreadful distance thou standest from that charity, which hopeth, believeth, and beareth all things; and from that humility, which, in a truly contrite heart, knoweth no indignation nor resentment against any being but itself.

3. It is so far from being difficult to live in peace with the gentle and the good, that it is highly grateful to all that are inclined to cultivate peace; for we naturally love those most, whose sentiments and dispositions correspond most with our own; but to maintain peace with the churlish and perverse, the irregular and impatient, and those that most contradict and oppose our opinions and desires, is an heroic and glorious attainment, which only an extraordinary measure of grace can enable us to acquire.

4. But there are some, that preserve the peace of their own breasts, and live in peace with all about them; and there are some, that having no peace in themselves, are continually employed in disturbing the peace of others: they are the tormentors of their brethren, and still more the tormentors of their own hearts; there are also some, who not only retain their own peace, but make it their principal business to restore peace to all that want it. After all, however, the most perfect peace to which we can attain in this miserable life, consists rather in meek and patient suffering, than in an exemption from adversity; and he that has most learned to suffer, will certainly possess the greatest share of peace; he is the conqueror of himself, the lord of the world, the friend of Christ, and the heir of heaven!

4

Of Simplicity and Purity

1. SIMPLICITY and purity are the two wings, with which man soars above the earth and all temporary nature. Simplicity is in the intention; purity, in the affection: simplicity turns to God; purity unites with and enjoys him.

2. No good action will be difficult and painful, if thou wert free from inordinate affection; and this internal freedom thou wilt then enjoy, when it is the one simple intention of thy mind to obey the will of God, and do good to thy fellow-creatures.

3. If thy heart was rightly disposed, every creature would be a book of divine knowledge: a mirror of life, in which thou mightest contemplate the eternal power and beneficence of the author of life: for there is no creature, however small and abject, that is not a monument of the goodness of God.

4. Such as is the frame of the spirit, such is its perception and judgment of outward things. If thou hadst simplicity and purity, thou wouldst be able to comprehend all things without error, and behold them without danger: the pure heart safely pervades, not only heaven, but hell.

5. If there be joy in this world, who possesses it more than the pure in heart? And if there be tribulation and anguish, who suffers them more than the wounded spirit?

6. As iron cast into the fire is purified from its rust, and becomes bright as the fire itself; so the soul, that in simplicity and purity turns and adheres to God, is delivered from the corruption of animal nature, and changed unto the "new man," formed "after the image of him who created him."

7. Those who suffer the desire of perfection to grow cold and languid, are terrified at the most inconsiderable difficulties, and soon driven back to seek consolation in the enjoyments of sensual life; but those, in whom that desire is kept alive and invigorated by continual self-denial, and a steady perseverance in that narrow path in which Christ has called us to follow him, find every step they take more and more easy, and feel those labours light that were once thought insurmountable.

5

Of Personal Attention

1. WE ought to place but little confidence in ourselves, because we are often destitute both of grace and understanding. The light we have is small, and that is soon lost by negligence. We are even insensible of this inward darkness: we do wrong and aggravate our guilt by excusing it; we are impelled by passion, and mistake it for zeal; we severely reprove little failings in our brethren, and pass over enormous sins in ourselves; we quickly feel, and perpetually brood over the sufferings that are brought upon us by others, but have no thought of what others suffer from us. If, however, a man would but truly and impartially examine himself, he would find but little cause to judge severely of his neighbour.

2. The spiritual man prefers to all other cares, the care of his own improvement; and he that is strictly watchful over his own conduct, will easily be silent about the conduct of others. But to the divine life of the spiritual man thou wilt never attain, unless

thou canst withdraw thy attention from all persons, and the concerns of all, and fix it wholly upon thyself. He that purely and simply intends and desires only the re-union of his soul with God, will not easily be moved by what he hears or sees in the world.

3. Tell me, if thou canst, where thou hast been wandering, when thou art absent from thy own breast: and after thou hast run about, and taken a hasty view of the actions and affairs of men, what advantage bringest thou home to thy neglected and forsaken self? He that desires peace of heart, and re-union with the divine nature, must cast all persons and things behind him, and keep God and his own spirit only in his view.

4. As thy progress to perfection depends much upon thy freedom from the cares and pleasures of the world, it must be proportionably obstructed by whatever degree of value they have in thy affections. Abandon, therefore, all hope of consolation from created things, not only as vain, but dangerous; and esteem nothing honourable, nothing pleasing, nothing great and worthy the desire of an immortal spirit, but God, and that which immediately tends to the improvement of thy state in him. The soul that truly loves God, despises all that is inferior to God. It is God alone, the Infinite and Eternal, who filleth all things, that is the life, light, and peace of all blessed spirits.

6

Of the Joy of a Good Conscience

1. THE "rejoicing" of a good man is "the testimony of his conscience." A pure conscience is the ground of perpetual exultation: it will support a man under the severest trials, and enable him to rejoice in the depths of adversity: but an evil conscience, in every state of life, is full of disquietude and fear. Thou wilt always enjoy tranquillity, if thy heart condemn thee not.

2. Do not hope to rejoice but when thou hast done well. The wicked cannot have true joy, nor taste of inward peace: for "there is no peace to the wicked," saith the Lord: "but they are like the troubled sea when it cannot rest, whose waters cast up mire and dirt." If they say, "We are in peace; no evil shall come upon us; and who will dare to hurt us?" believe them not; for the anger of the Lord will suddenly rise up within them; and their boasting shall vanish like smoke, and the thoughts of their hearts shall perish.

3. To "glory in tribulation," is not difficult to him that loveth; for thus to glory, is "to glory in the cross of our Lord Jesus Christ." That glory is short and painful, which is given and received among men: it comes with fear and envy, and vanishes in disappointment and regret. The glory of the just is proclaimed by the voice of conscience, and not by the mouth of men: their joy is from God, and in God; and their rejoicing is founded in truth. He that aspires after true and eternal glory, values not that which is temporal; and he that seeketh after the temporal glory of the earth, or that does not despise it from his heart, proves, that he neither loves nor considers the eternal glory of heaven.

4. He only can have great tranquillity, whose happiness depends not on the praise or dispraise of men. If thy conscience were pure, thou wouldst be contented in every condition, and undisturbed by the opinions and reports of men concerning thee; for their commendations can add nothing to thy holiness, nor their censures take any thing from it: what thou art, thou art; nor can the praise of the whole world make thee greater in the sight of God. The more, therefore, thy attention is fixed upon the true state of thy spirit, the less wilt thou regard what is said of thee in the world. Men look only on the face, but God looketh on and searcheth the heart; men consider only the outward act, but God the inward principle from which it springs.

5. To think of having done well without self-esteem, is an evidence of true humility; as it is of great inward purity and faith, to abandon the hope of consolation from created things. He that seeketh not a witness for himself among men, shows that he

has committed his whole state to God, the witness in his own breast: for it is "not he who commendeth himself," nor he who is commended by others, that "is approved;" but him only, saith the blessed Paul, "whom God commendeth."

6. To walk in the presence of God manifested in the heart, and not to be enslaved by any worldly affection, is the state of the internal man.

7

Of the Love of Jesus above All

1. Blessed is the man who knoweth what it is to love Jesus, and for his sake to despise himself. To preserve this love, thou must relinquish the love of thyself and all creatures: for Jesus will be loved alone. The love of the creatures is deceitful and unstable; the love of Jesus is faithful and permanent. He that adhereth to any creature, must fail when the creature faileth; but he that adhereth to Jesus, will be established with him for ever. Love him and cherish his love, who, though the heavens and the earth should be dissolved, will not forsake thee, nor suffer thee to perish. Thou must one day be separated from all that thou seest and lovest among created things, whether thou wilt or not: living and dying, therefore, adhere to Jesus, and securely commit thyself to his faithful protection, who, when all temporal nature fails, is alone able to sustain thee.

2. Such is the purity of thy beloved, that he will admit of no rival for thy love, but will himself have the sole possession of thy

heart, and, like a king, reign there with sovereign authority, as on his proper throne.

3. If thy heart was emptied of self-love, and of the love of creatures whom thou lovest only for thy own sake, Jesus would dwell with thee continually. But whatever love thou hast for men, of which Jesus is not the principal and end, and whatever be their returns of love to thee, thou wilt find both to be utterly vain and worthless. O place not thy confidence in man; lean not upon a hollow reed! For "all flesh is as grass, and all the glory of man as the flower of grass; the grass withereth, and the flower thereof falleth away."

4. Of men thou regardest only the outward appearance, and, therefore, art soon deceived; and while thou seekest relief and comfort from them, thou must meet with disappointment and distress. If in all things thou seekest only Jesus, thou wilt surely find him in all; and if thou seekest thyself, thou wilt, indeed, find thyself, but to thy own destruction: for he who in all things seeks not Jesus alone, involves himself in more evil, than the world and all his enemies could heap upon him.

8

Of the Friendship of Jesus

1. WHEN Jesus is present, all is well, and no labour seems difficult: but when he is absent, the least adversity is found insupportable. When Jesus is silent, all comfort withers away; but the moment he speaks again, though but a single word, the soul rises from her distress, and feels her comfort revive in greater power. Thus Mary rose hastily from the place where she sat weeping for the death of Lazarus, when Martha said to her, "The Master is come, and calleth for thee." Blessed is the hour, when Jesus calls us from affliction and tears, to partake of the joys of his spirit!

2. How great is the aridity and hardness of thy heart, without Jesus: how great its vanity and folly, when it desireth any good but him! Is not the loss of him greater than the loss of the world? For what can the world profit thee, without Jesus? To be without Jesus, is to be in the depths of hell: to be with him,

is to be in paradise. While Jesus is with thee, no enemy hath power to hurt thee. He that findeth Jesus, findeth a treasure of infinite value, a good transcending all that can be called good; and he that loseth Jesus, loseth more than the whole world: for he loseth the heavenly life and light of his own soul. That man only is poor in this world, who liveth without Jesus; and that man only is rich, with whom Jesus delights to dwell.

3. It requires great skill to converse with Jesus, and great wisdom to know how to keep him; but not the skill of men, nor the wisdom of this world. Be humble and peaceful, and Jesus will come to thee; be devout and meek, and he will dwell with thee. But thou mayest soon drive away Jesus from thy heart, and lose the grace which he has given thee, by turning aside to the enjoyments of the world: and when thou hast driven him away and lost him, to whom wilt thou then fly? And where wilt thou find a friend? Without a friend, life is unenjoyed; and unless Jesus be thy chosen friend, infinitely loved and preferred above all others, life will be to thee a scene of desolation and distress. It is madness, therefore, to place thy confidence and delight in any other: rather choose that the whole world should combine to oppose and injure thee, than that Jesus should be offended at thy preferring the world to him. Of all that are dear to thee, then, let Jesus be the peculiar and supreme object of thy love. Men, even those to whom thou art united by the ties of nature, and the reciprocations of friendship, are to be loved only for the sake of Jesus: but Jesus is to be loved for himself: Jesus alone is to be loved without reserve, and without measure; because, of all that we can possibly love, he alone is infinite in goodness and faithfulness. For his sake, and in the power of his love, thy enemies are to be dear to

thee, as well as thy friends: and let it be thy continual prayer for all, even for thy enemies, that all may be blessed with the knowledge and love of him.

4. Do not desire to be admired and praised for the goodness that is in thee, as if it was thy own; for the praise of being good, is the prerogative of God: his goodness alone is absolute and underived; and thou art good, only by the communication of that goodness, which from eternity to eternity dwells essentially in him. Neither desire to engage the affections of any particular person, nor suffer thy own affections to be engaged by any: but let it be thy sole wish and joy, to have Jesus dwell in thy own heart, and the hearts of all others, as the eternal life, light, and peace of all.

5. Aspire after such inward purity and freedom, that no affection to any creature may have power to perplex and enslave thee: thou must have a heart divested of all selfish affections, and earthly desires, before thou wilt be able, in peaceful vacancy, to "stand still, and see the salvation of the Lord." Indeed, to this exalted state thou canst not arrive, without the prevention and attraction of his grace; which, by delivering thee from all attachment to created life, will bring thee into union with his blessed Spirit, and he will be one with thee, and thou with him.

6. When the grace of God thus liveth and reigneth in the heart of man, he hath power to "do all things:" but when its divine influence is suspended, he feels himself left in the poverty and weakness of fallen nature, exposed to the lash of every affliction. Yet, in this forlorn and desolate state, thou must not

despair; but with a calm and meek spirit resign thyself to the divine will, and for the glory of Christ, patiently bear whatever befalls thee; remembering that winter is invariably succeeded by summer, night by day, and darkness and tempest by serenity and sunshine.

9

Of the Disconsolate State

1. IT requries no considerable effort to despise human consolation, when we are possessed of divine: but it is transcendent greatness, to bear the want of both; and, without self-condolence, or the least retrospection on our own imaginary worth, patiently to suffer "desolation of heart" for the glory of God. What singular attainment is it, to be peaceful and devout, while "the light of God's countenance is lifted up upon thee?" For this is the hour that all creatures most desire. That man cannot but find his journey easy and delightful, whom the grace of God sustains: and what wonder, if he neither feels burthen, nor meets with obstruction, when he is supported by omnipotence, and conducted by truth.

2. We perpetually seek after consolation, from the dread of the want of it; and it is with difficulty that man is so far divested of self, as not to seek it in his earthly and selfish state. The holy

martyr, Laurence, overcame the world and himself, in subduing his great affection for his good bishop, Xystus: for, though all that was delightful to him in this life, centered in their personal endearments; yet, with calm resolution he bore a sudden and violent separation from him, to which death only could put an end. By the love of God, therefore, he overcame the love of man, and steadily preferred the divine will to the comforts of human converse. With the same patient resignation, must thou also, for the love of God, learn to part with thy dearest and most intimate friend. And some argument against impatient sorrow at such events, may be drawn from the inevitable mortality which sin has introduced; under whose universal dominion it must be the trial of every man, to be separated from that which in this world he held most dear.

3. It requires long and severe conflicts to subdue the earthly and selfish nature, and turn all the desire of the soul to God. He that trusts to his own wisdom and strength, is easily seduced to seek repose in human consolation: but he that truly loves Christ, and depends only upon his redeeming power within him, as the principle of holiness and truth, turns not aside to such vain comforts, nor, indeed, seeks after any of the delights of sense; but rather chooses the severe exercises of self-denial, and, for the sake of Christ, to endure the most painful labours.

4. When, therefore, God bestows upon thee the consolations of the Spirit, receive them with all thankfulness; but remember, they are his gift, not thy desert; and instead of being elate, careless, and presuming, be more humble, more watchful and devout in all thy conduct: for the hour of light and peace will soon pass

away, and darkness and temptation will succeed. Yet, when this awful change intervenes, do not immediately despair, but with humility and patience wait for the return of the heavenly visitation; for God, who is infinite in goodness as well as in power, is both able and willing to renew the bounties of his grace in more abundant measures.

5. The vicissitude of day and night in the spiritual life, is neither new nor unexpected to those that are acquainted with the ways of God; for the ancient prophets and most eminent saints have all experienced an alternative of visitation and desertion. As an instance of this the royal prophet thus describes his own case: "When I was in prosperity," says he, and my heart was filled with the treasures of grace, I said, "I shall never be moved." But these treasures being soon taken away, and feeling in himself the poverty of fallen nature, he adds, "thou didst turn thy face from me and I was troubled." Yet in this disconsolate state he does not despair; but with more ardour raises his desire and prayer to God: "Unto thee, O Lord, will I cry, and I will make my supplication unto my God." He then testifies, that his prayer is accepted, and his prosperous state restored; "The Lord hath heard me, and hath had mercy upon me; the Lord is become my helper." And to show how this mercy and help were manifested, he adds, "Thou hast turned my mourning into joy, and hast compassed me about with gladness." And if this interchange of light and darkness, joy and sorrow, was the common state of the greatest saints; surely, such poor and infirm creatures as we are, ought not to despair, when we are sometimes elevated by fervour: and sometimes depressed by coldness; for the Holy Spirit cometh and goeth, "according to the good pleasure of his will:" and upon this principle

the blessed Job saith; "Thou visitest man in the morning, and of a sudden thou provest him."

6. In what, therefore, can I hope, or where ought I to place my confidence, but in infinite goodness, and the life, light, and peace of the Divine Spirit? For whether the conversation of holy men, the endearing kindness of faithful friends, the melody of music in psalms and hymns, the entertainment of ingenious books, nay, the instructions of the oracles of God; whether any or all these advantages are present, what do they all avail, what joy can they dispense, when the Holy Spirit is withdrawn from my soul, and I am left to the poverty and wretchedness of my fallen self? In such a state, no remedy remains but meek and humble patience, and the total surrender of my will to the blessed will of God.

7. I never yet found a man so invariably holy and devout, as not to have experienced the absence of grace, and felt some decay of spiritual fervour: and from this severe trial no saint has been exempt, to whatever degrees of rapture and elevation his spirit may have been exalted. It is a trial, however, that when patiently endured for the love of God, prepares and qualifies the soul for the high state of divine contemplation. It may always be considered also as the sign of approaching comfort; and to those who suffer it with resignation, humility, and faith, is the uninterrupted felicity of Paradise chiefly promised: "To him that overcometh," saith He who is "the First and the Last, will I give to eat of the tree of life, which is in the midst of the Paradise of God."

8. The ground of this vicissitude of comfort and distress, is, in general, this: the consolations of the Spirit are given to man,

to enable him to bear the adversity of his fallen state; and they are taken away, lest he be so much elevated with the gift, as to forget the giver.

9. After all, remember, that the devil slumbereth not, nor is the flesh yet dead: be, therefore, continually prepared for contest; for, on the right hand, and on the left, thou art beset with enemies that are never at rest.

10

Of True Thankfulness for
the Grace of God

1. WHY seekest thou rest, when thou art born to labour? Dispose thyself for patience, rather than for consolation; rather for bearing the cross, than for receiving joy.

2. Who among those that are devoted to the world, would not gladly receive the joys and consolations of the Spirit, if they could be obtained without relinquishing the pursuits of honour, wealth and pleasure? The joys and consolations of the Spirit transcend the delights of the world and the pleasures of sense, as far as heaven transcends the earth: these are either impure or vain; those alone are holy, substantial, delightful; the fruits of that new nature which is born of God. But those no man can enjoy at what time, and in what measure he pleases; and he finds, that the seasons of temptation return soon and last long.

3. False freedom and self-confidence greatly oppose the heavenly visitation. God, who is infinite in goodness, manifests that goodness, in bestowing the gift of his Holy Spirit; man, who is wholly evil, shows that evil, in not rendering back the gift with the thankfulness and praise of dependant wretchedness; the power of the gift is destroyed by ingratitude to the giver: the course of grace is stopped, by diverting and confining its streams, and not suffering them to flow back to their divine source. For the influences of God's Spirit are in large measures poured only upon the truly thankful, and from the proud is taken away that which is always given to the humble.

4. I wish for no consolation that robs me of compunction; nor aim at any contemplation that will exalt me into pride; for every thing that is high, is not holy; nor every desire pure; nor every thing that is sweet good; nor every thing that is dear to man, pleasing to God. But acceptable, beyond measure, is that grace by which I am made more humble and fearful, and more disposed to deny and renounce myself: for he that hath experienced the divine gift, and been taught the infinite value of it, by feeling its loss, so far from daring to appropriate any thing good to himself, will in the deepest humility acknowledge and lament the poverty and nakedness of his fallen spirit. "Render, therefore, unto God, that which is God's," and take to thyself that which is properly thy own; give him the glory of all thy good, and leave for thyself only the shame and punishment of all thy evil.

5. Set thyself in the lowest place, and the highest shall be given thee; for the more lofty the building is designed to be, the deeper

must the foundations of it be laid. The greatest saints in the sight of God, are the least in their own esteem; and the height of their glory is always in proportion to the depth of their humility. Those that are filled with true and heavenly glory, have no place for the desire of that which is earthly and vain; being rooted and established in God, they cannot possibly be lifted up in self-exaltation. Whatever good they have, they acknowledge it to be received; and ascribing the glory of it to the supreme author of good, they "seek not honour one of another, but the honour that cometh from God alone;" and that God may be glorified in himself, and in all his saints, is the prevailing desire of their hearts, and the principal end of all their actions.

6. Be thankful for what thou receivest, and thou wilt be deemed worthy to receive more. Let that which is thought the least of God's gifts, be unto thee even as the greatest; and that which is held contemptible, as a singular favour. The dignity of the giver confers dignity on all his gifts; and none can be small, that is bestowed by the supreme God. Even pain and punishment from him are to be gratefully received; for whatever he permitteth to befal us, he permitteth it to promote the important business of our redemption. Let him, therefore, that desireth to preserve the grace of God in his heart, be thankful when it is given, and patient when it is taken away; let him pray ardently for its return; and be particularly watchful and humble, that he may lose it no more.

11

Of the Small Number of Those That Love the Cross

1. JESUS hath now many lovers of his heavenly kingdom, but few bearers of his cross; he hath many that desire to partake of his comforts, but few that are willing to share in his distress; he finds many companions of his table, but few of his hours of abstinence. All are disposed to rejoice with Jesus, but few to suffer sorrow for his sake: many follow him to the breaking of bread, but few to the drinking of his bitter cup; many attend with reverence on the glory of his miracles, but few follow the ignominy of his cross. Many love Jesus, while they are free from adversity; many praise and bless him, while they receive his consolations: but if Jesus hide his face, and leave them but a little, their confidence and their devotion vanish, and they sink either into murmur or despair.

2. But they who love Jesus for himself, and not for their own personal comfort, will bless him in the depths of tribulation and

distress, as well as in the most exalted state of consolation. Nay, should he continue to withhold his consolations from them, they would still continue to praise him, still give him thanks. O mighty power of the pure love of Jesus, unadulterated with any base mixture of self-love and self-interest! Do not they deserve the name of hirelings, who are forever seeking after comfort? Do not all prove, that they are lovers of themselves, more than lovers of Christ, who desire and think of nothing, but the repose and pleasure of their own minds?

3. Where is the man that serveth God, without the hope of reward? Where, indeed, is that true poverty of spirit to be found, which is divested of all that is thought rich and valuable in the creatures and self? This is "the pearl of great price," that is worthy to be sought after to the utmost bounds of nature! Though a man give all his substance to feed the poor, it is nothing; though he mortify the desires of flesh and blood by severe penance, still it is of little importance; though he comprehend the vast extent of science, yet he is far behind; and though he hath the splendour of illustrious virtue, and the ardour of exalted devotion, still he will want much, if he still wants this "one thing needful," this poverty of spirit, which, after abandoning the creatures about him, requires him to abandon himself; to go wholly out of himself; to retain not the least leaven of self-love and self-esteem; but, when he hath finished his course of duty, to know and feel, with the same certainty as he feels the motion of his heart, that he himself hath done nothing.

4. Such a man will set no value upon those attainments, which, if under the power of self-love, he would highly esteem; but, in

concurrence with the voice of truth, "when he has done all that is commanded him," he will always freely pronounce himself "an unprofitable servant." This is that poverty and nakedness of spirit, which can say with the Psalmist: Lord, in myself, "I am poor and desolate!" And yet there is none so rich, none so free, none so powerful, as he, who, renouncing himself and all creatures, can remain peaceable in the most abject state of abasement.

12

Of the Necessity of Bearing the Cross

1. THIS saying seems hard to all: "Deny thyself, take up thy cross and follow me." But as hard a saying will be heard, when the same divine voice shall pronounce, "Depart from me, ye cursed, into everlasting fire!" They, therefore, who can now attentively hear, and patiently follow the call to bear the cross, will not be terrified at the sentence of the final judgment. In that awful day the banner of the cross will be displayed in heaven; and all who have conformed their lives to Christ crucified, will draw near to Christ the judge, with holy confidence. Why, then, dost thou fear to take up the cross, which will direct thee to the path that leads to the kingdom of God?

2. In the cross is life, in the cross is health, in the cross is protection from every enemy; from the cross are derived heavenly meekness, true fortitude, the joys of the Spirit, the conquest of self, the perfection of holiness! There is no redemption, no

foundation for the hope of the divine life, but in the cross. Take up thy cross, therefore, and follow Jesus, in the path that leads to everlasting peace. He hath gone before, bearing that cross upon which he died for thee, that thou mightest follow, patiently bearing thy own cross, and upon that die to thyself for him; and if we die with him, we shall also live with him; "if we are partakers of his sufferings, we shall be partakers also of his glory."

3. Behold, all consists in the death of self upon the cross; and there is no means to obtain life and peace, but by daily dying upon the cross to all the appetites and passions of fallen nature! Go where thou wilt, seek after what methods thou pleasest to accomplish thy redemption, thou canst not find a sublimer way above, nor a more secure way below, than this of dying upon the cross.

4. Though thou disposest all thy affairs according to thy own fancy, and conductest them by the dictates of thy own judgment, still thou wilt continually meet with some evil, which thou must necessarily bear, either with, or against thy will; and, therefore, wilt continually find the cross; thou wilt feel either pain of body, or distress and anguish of spirit. Sometimes thou wilt experience the absence of grace; sometimes thy neighbour will put thy meekness and patience to the test; and, what is more than this, thou wilt sometimes feel a burthen in thyself, which no human help can remove, no earthly comfort lighten; but bear it thou must, as long as it is the will of God to continue it upon thee. It is the blessed will of God in permitting no ray of comfort to visit us in the darkness of distress, that we should

learn such profound humility and submission, as to resign our whole state, present and future, to his absolute disposal.

5. No heart can have so true a sense of the sufferings of Christ, as that which has suffered in the same kind. The cross is always ready, and waits for thee in every place. Run where thou wilt, thou canst not avoid it; for wherever thou runnest, thou takest thyself with thee, and art always sure of finding thyself. Turn which way thou wilt, either to the things above, or the things below; to that which is within, or that which is without thee; thou wilt in all certainly find the cross; and if thou wouldst enjoy peace, and obtain the unfading crown of glory, it is necessary that in every place, and in all events, thou shouldst bear it willingly, and "in patience possess thy soul."

6. If thou bearest the cross willingly, it will soon bear thee, and lead thee beyond the reach of suffering, where "God shall take away all sorrow from thy heart." But if thou bearest it with reluctance, it will be a burthen to thee inexpressibly painful, which yet thou must still feel; and by every impatient effort to throw it from thee, thou wilt only render thyself less and less able to sustain its weight, till at length, it crush thee.

7. Why hopest thou to avoid that from which no human being has been exempt? Who among the saints hath accomplished his pilgrimage in this world, without adversity and distress? Even our blessed Lord passed not one hour of his most holy life, without tasting "the bitter cup that was given him to drink;" and, of himself, he saith, that "it behoved him to suffer, and to rise from the dead, and so to enter into his glory." And why dost thou seek any other path to glory, but that, in which, bearing the cross,

thou art called to follow "the captain of thy salvation?" The life of Christ was a continual cross, an unbroken chain of sufferings; and desirest thou a perpetuity of repose and joy? Thou art deceived, wretchedly deceived, if thou expectest any thing but tribulation; for this mortal life is full of misery, and every part of it is inscribed with the cross.

8. The regenerate man, as he becomes more spiritualized, has a quicker discernment of the cross wherever it meets him; and his sense of the evils of his exile, as the punishment of his fallen life, increases in proportion to his love of God, and desire of re-union with him. But this man, thus sensible of misery, derives hope even from his sufferings; for while he sustains them with meek and humble submission, their weight is continually diminishing; and what to carnal minds is the object of terror, is to him a pledge of heavenly comfort. He feels that the strength, the life and peace of the new man, rise from the troubles, the decay and death of the old; and from his desire of conformity to his crucified Saviour, as the only means of restoration to his first perfect state in God, he derives so much strength and comfort under the severest tribulations, that he wisheth not to live a moment without them. Of the truth of this the blessed Paul is an illustrious instance; who says of himself, "I take pleasure in infirmities, in reproaches, in necessities, in persecutions, in distresses for Christ's sake; for when I am weak, then am I strong."

9. This desire of suffering, however, and this meek and patient submission under it, is not the effect of any power which is inherent in man, and which he can boast of as his own; but is the pure fruit of the grace of Christ, operating so powerfully in the

fallen soul, as to make it love and embrace that which it would naturally abhor and shun. No; it is not in man to love and to bear the cross; to resist the appetites of the body, and bring them under absolute subjection to the spirit; to shun honours; to receive affronts with meekness; to despise himself, and to wish to be despised by others; to bear, with calm resignation, the loss of fortune, health and friends; and to have no desire after the riches, the honours and pleasures of the world. If thou dependest upon thy own will and strength to do and to suffer all this, thou wilt find thyself as unable to accomplish it as to create another world; but if thou turnest to the divine power within thee, and trustest only to that as the doer and sufferer of all, the strength of omnipotence will be imparted to thee, and the world and the flesh shall be put under thy feet; armed with this holy confidence, and defended by the cross of Christ, thou needest not fear the most malignant efforts of thy great adversary the devil.

10. Dispose thyself, therefore, like a true and faithful servant, to bear with fortitude and resolution the cross of thy blessed Lord, to which he was nailed in testimony of his infinite love of thee. Prepare thy spirit to suffer patiently the innumerable inconveniences and troubles of this miserable life; for these thou wilt find, though thou runnest to the ends of the earth, or hidest thyself in its deepest caverns; and it is patient suffering alone, that can either disarm their power, or heal the wounds they have made. Drink freely and affectionately of thy Lord's bitter cup, if thou desirest to manifest thy friendship for him, and "the part thou hast with him." Resign to the will of God the dispensation of his comforts, and wish only for tribulation, in its innumerable forms, as the choicest blessing of thy earthly life; for "the sufferings of the present time," if they

were all accumulated for thy portion, "are not worthy to be compared with the glory which shall be revealed in thee."

11. When thou hast obtained so true a conquest over self-love, that the love of Christ shall make tribulation not only easy but desirable; then all will be well with thee, and thou wilt have found the gate of paradise: but while every tribulation is painful and grievous, and it is the desire of thy soul to avoid it, thou canst not but be wretched, and what thou labourest to shun will follow thee wherever thou goest. The patient enduring of the cross, and the death of self upon it, are the indispensable duty of fallen man; and it is by these alone that he can be delivered from his darkness, corruption and misery, and restored to the possession of life, light and peace. Though, like St. Paul, thou wert caught up to the third heaven, yet thou wouldst not be exempt from suffering: for of St. Paul himself, his Redeemer said, "I will show him how great things he must suffer for my name's sake." To suffer, therefore, is thy portion; and to suffer patiently and willingly, is the great testimony of thy love and allegiance to thy Lord.

12. O that thou wert worthy to suffer any affliction for the name of Jesus! What glory would be laid up in store for thyself, what joy would be diffused among the saints of God, what holy emulation excited in thy neighbour! Though patience is extolled by all, yet few are willing to suffer: but thou mayest well suffer a little for Christ, when men endure so much for the world.

13. Know, that thy life must be a continual death to the appetites and passions of fallen nature; and know also, that the more

perfectly thou diest to thyself, the more truly wilt thou begin to live to God. No man is qualified to understand the stupendous truths of redemption, till he has subdued his impatience and self-love, and is ready to suffer any adversity for the sake of Christ. This is so acceptable to God, and so beneficial to the soul, that if the condition of thy present life was left to thy own choice, thou shouldst prefer suffering affliction for the sake of Christ, to the uninterrupted enjoyment of repose and comfort; for this will render thee conformable to Christ and all his saints. Indeed, the perfection of our state, and our acceptableness with God, depend more upon the patient suffering of long and severe distress, than upon continual consolation and ecstasy.

14. If any way, but bearing the cross and dying to his own will, could have redeemed man from that fallen life of self in flesh and blood, which is his alienation from, and enmity to God; Christ would have taught it in his word, and established it by his example. But of all universally that desire to follow him, he has required the bearing of the cross; and without exception he has said to all, "If any man will come after me, let him deny himself, take up his cross, and follow me."

15. When, therefore, we have read all books, and examined all methods, to find out the path that will lead us back to the blessed state from which we have wandered, this conclusion only will remain, "that through much tribulation we must enter into the kingdom of God."

BOOK III

Of Divine Illumination

1

Of the Blessedness of Internal Conversation with Christ

DISCIPLE

1. I WILL hear what the Lord my God will say within me.

CHRIST

Blessed is the soul that listeneth to the voice of the Lord, and from his own lips heareth the word of consolation! Blessed are the ears that receive the soft whispers of the divine breath, and exclude the noise and tumult of the world; yea, truly blessed are they, when deaf to the voice that soundeth without, they are attentive only to the truth teaching within! Blessed are the eyes that are shut to material objects, and open and fixed upon those that are spiritual! Blessed are they that examine the state of the internal man; and, by continual exercises of repentance and faith, prepare the mind for a more comprehensive knowledge of the truths of redemption! Blessed are all who delight in the service of God; and who, that they may live purely to him, disengage their hearts from the cares and pleasures of the world!

DISCIPLE

2. Consider these transcendent blessings, O my soul! and perpetually exclude the objects of sensual desire, that thou mayest be able to hear and understand the voice of the Lord thy God! Thy beloved speaketh again.

CHRIST

I am thy life, thy peace, and thy salvation: keep thyself united to me, and thou shalt find rest. Remove far from thee the transitory enjoyments of earth, and desire and seek after the eternal enjoyments prepared for thee in heaven: for what are those transitory enjoyments, but delusions and snares? And what can all creatures avail thee, when thou hast forsaken the Creator? Abandon, therefore, all created things, that, by a faithful and pure adherence, thou mayest be acceptable to him in whom thou hast thy being, and in union with his Spirit, enjoy everlasting felicity.

2

That Christ, Who Is the Truth, Speaketh to the Soul, without the Sound of Words; That His Instructions Are to Be Heard with Humility; and That Many Regard Them Not

DISCIPLE

1. "SPEAK, Lord, for thy servant heareth." "I am thy servant; give me understanding, that I may know thy testimonies. Incline my heart to the words of thy mouth;" "let thy speech distil as the dew!"

2. The children of Israel once said to Moses, "speak thou with us, and we will hear: let not God speak with us, lest we die." I pray not in this manner: no, Lord, I pray not so; but, with the prophet Samuel, humbly and ardently entreat, "Speak, Lord, for thy servant heareth. Let not Moses speak to me, nor any of the

prophets; but speak thou, O Lord God, the inspirer and enlightener of all the prophets; for thou alone, without their intervention, canst perfectly instruct me; but, without thee, they can profit me nothing. They, indeed, can pronounce the words, but cannot impart the Spirit: they may entertain the fancy with the charms of eloquence, but, if thou art silent, they do not inflame the heart. They administer the letter, but thou openest the sense; they utter the mystery, but thou revealest its meaning; they publish thy laws, but thou conferrest the power of obedience; they point out the way to life, but thou bestowest strength to walk in it: their influence is only external, but thou instructest and enlightenest the mind; they water, but thou givest the increase; their voice soundeth in the ear, but it is thou that givest understanding to the heart.

3. Let not, therefore, Moses speak: but do thou, O Lord my God, Eternal Truth! Speak to my soul; lest, being only outwardly warned, but not inwardly quickened, I die, and be found unfruitful: lest the word heard and not obeyed, known and not loved, professed and not kept, turn to my condemnation. "Speak," therefore, Lord, "for thy servant heareth;" "thou" only "hast the words of eternal life:" O speak to the comfort of my soul, to the renovation of my heavenly nature, and to the eternal praise and glory of thy own holy name.

CHRIST

4. Son, hear my words: words full of heavenly sweetness, infinitely transcending the learning and eloquence of all the philosophers and wise men of this world. "The words that I speak, they are spirit and they are life;" not to be weighed

in the balance of human understanding, nor perverted to the indulgence of vain curiosity; but to be heard in silence, and received with meek simplicity, and ardent affection.

DISCIPLE

"Blessed is the man, whom thou instructest, O Lord, and teachest him out of thy law; that thou mayest give him rest from the days of adversity," lest he be left desolate upon the earth.

CHRIST

5. I taught the prophets from the beginning, and even till now cease not to speak unto all; but many are deaf to my voice. Most men listen more attentively to the world than to God; they more readily submit to the painful tyranny of sensual appetites, than to the mild and sanctifying restraints of God's holy will. The world promiseth only impure and transitory joy, and men engage with ardour in its unholy service; I promise that which is supreme and everlasting, and their hearts are insensible and unmoved. Where is the man that serveth and obeyeth me, with that affection and solicitude, with which the world and the rulers of it are served and obeyed? Even the sea exclaimeth, "be thou ashamed, O Zidon!" Because, for a trifling acquisition of wealth or honour, a tedious and fatiguing journey is cheerfully undertaken; but, to obtain eternal life, not a foot is lifted from the earth. The sordid gain of perishing riches, engages the pursuit, and employs the industry of all; the most inconsiderable share of this imaginary property is obstinately and bitterly contested. For the vain expectation of a vainer possession, men dread not the fatigue of sleepless nights and restless days: but, deplorable insensibility! For unchangeable good, for an inestimable recompense, for unsullied

glory and endless happiness, the least solicitude and the least labour is thought too dear a purchase.

6. Be ashamed, therefore, O slothful and discontented servant, that the children of the world should with more ardour seek after destruction and death, than thou to obtain eternal life; that they should rejoice more in vanity, than thou in the truth. Their hope is, indeed, vain, as that on which it is erected; but the hope that dependeth on my promises, is never sent empty away; to all that faithfully persevere in my love, what I have promised I will give, what I have said I will fulfil. "I am the rewarder of them that diligently seek me: I am he which searcheth" and trieth "the hearts" of the devout.

7. Write my words upon thy heart; ponder them day and night: in the time of trouble thou wilt find their truth and efficacy: and what thou now readest and understandest not, the day of temptation will explain. I visit man, both by trials and comforts; and continually read him two lessons, one to rebuke his selfishness and impurity, and the other to excite him to the pursuit of holiness. He that hath my word and despiseth it, hath that which "shall judge him in the last day."

3

The Soul Imploring the Influence of Grace, Is Instructed to Walk before God in Humility and Truth

DISCIPLE

1. O LORD my God, thou art my supreme and consummate good! And what am I, that I should presume to open my lips before thee? I am thy least and most unprofitable servant; an abject worm; much more poor and contemptible than I dare to express, or am able to conceive! Yet remember me, O Lord, and have mercy upon me; for, without thee I have nothing, can do nothing, and am nothing. Thou alone art just and holy, and good; thy power is infinite, and the manifestations of it boundless; thou fillest all things, except the heart of the impenitent sinner, that obstinately rejects the offers of thy redeeming love. Remember, O Lord, the love that brought me into being; and as thou madest all things for the communication of thy perfections and blessedness, O fill me with thyself!

2. How can I sustain the darkness and misery of this fallen life, unless thy truth enlighten me, and thy strength support me! O turn not thy face from me, delay not thy fatherly visitation, suspend not the consolations of thy spirit, lest my soul become like a barren and thirsty land where no water is! Lord "teach me to do thy will;" teach me to walk before thee in humility and faith, in fear and love! Thou art my wisdom, who knowest me in truth, and didst know me before I was born into the world, and before the world was made!

CHRIST

3. Son, walk before me in truth, and in singleness of heart seek me continually. He that walketh before me in truth shall be defended against the assaults of evil spirits, and delivered from the delusions and calumnies of wicked men. "If the truth make thee free, thou shalt be free indeed;" and shalt hear, without emotion, the vain commendations and censures of the world.

DISCIPLE

4. Lord, thy word is truth! As thou hast spoken, so, I beseech thee, be it done unto thy servant: let thy truth teach, protect, and preserve me to my final redemption; let it deliver me from every evil temper and inordinate desire, so shall I walk before thee in "the glorious liberty of the children of God!"

CHRIST

5. I will teach thee what is my "good, and acceptable, and perfect will." Think on the evil that is in thee, with deep compunction and self-abhorrence; and think on the good, without self-esteem and self-exaltation. In thyself thou art a wretched sinner, bound

with the complicated chain of many sensual and malignant passions. Thou art always tending to nothing and vanity; thou soon waverest, art soon subdued, soon disturbed, and easily seduced from the path of holiness and peace. There is in thee no good, which thou canst glory in as thy own; but much evil, as the ground of deep shame and self-abhorrence: thou art even more dark, corrupt, and powerless, than thou art able to comprehend.

6. Let not, therefore, pride deceive thee into false notions of the holiness and perfection of thy life; for thou hast nothing great, nothing valuable, nothing worthy of admiration and praise, nothing exalted, good, and desirable, but that which is produced by the operation of my Spirit. Let eternal truth be all thy comfort and thy boast, and thy own sinfulness, thy displeasure and thy shame. Fear, abhor, and shun nothing so much, as the evil tempers of thy fallen nature, and the evil habits of thy fallen life; which ought to offend and grieve thee more, than all the losses and distresses thou canst meet with in the world.

7. Some men walk not before me in simplicity and purity of heart; but moved by that curiosity and arrogance which deprived angels of heaven, and Adam of paradise, neglect themselves and their own salvation, to search into the counsels of infinite wisdom, and fathom the deep things of God. These fall into dangerous errors, and aggravated sins; and their pride and presumption I continually resist. But do thou fear the judgments of God; tremble at the wrath of Omnipotence; and, instead of questioning the proceedings of the Most High, search into the depths of thy own iniquities, that thou mayest know how much evil thou hast done, and how much good thou hast neglected.

8. Some place their religion in books, some in images, and some in the pomp and splendour of external worship; these honour "me with their lips, but their hearts is far from me." But there are some, that with illuminated understandings discern the glory which man has lost, and with pure affections pant for its recovery: these hear and speak with reluctance of the cares and pleasures of the present life, and even lament the necessity of administering to the wants of animal nature: these hear and understand what the Holy Spirit speaketh in their hearts, exhorting them to withdraw their affection from things on earth, and "set it on things above:" to abandon this fallen world, and day and night aspire after re-union with God.

4

Of the Power of Divine Love

1. I BLESS thee, O heavenly Father, the Father of my Lord Jesus Christ, that thou hast vouchsafed to remember so poor and helpless a creature! O Father of mercies, and God of all consolation, I give thee most humble and ardent thanks, that, unworthy as I am of all comfort, thou hast been pleased to visit my benighted soul with the enlivening beams of heavenly light! Blessing, and praise, and glory, be unto thee, and thy only begotten Son, and thy Holy Spirit, the Comforter, for ever and ever!

2. O Lord my God, who hast mercifully numbered me among the objects of thy redeeming love, when thou art pleased to visit me, all that is within me shall rejoice: for thou art my glory and my joy, my hope and refuge in the day of my distress. But because my love is yet feeble, and my holy resolutions imperfect,

I have continual need of thy strength and consolation: do thou, therefore, visit me continually, and instruct me out of thy law; deliver me from malignant passions, and sensual desires, that being healed and purified, I may love with more ardour, may suffer with more patience, may persevere with more constancy.

CHRIST

3. Love is, indeed, a transcendent excellence, an essential and sovereign good; it maketh the heavy burden light, and the rugged path smooth; it beareth all things without feeling their weight, and from every adversity taketh away the sting.

4. The love of Jesus is a noble and generous love, prompting to difficult attempts, and kindling the desire of greater perfection: it continually looketh up to heaven, and abhors the restraints of its earthly prison: it panteth after its original and native freedom; and, lest its intellectual eye should be darkened by earthly objects, and its will captivated by earthly good, or subdued by earthly evil, sighs for deliverance from this fallen world.

5. Love surpasseth all sweetness, strength, height, depth, and breadth; nothing is more pleasing, nothing more full, nothing more excellent, in heaven or in earth: for "love is born of God;" and it cannot find rest in created things, but resteth only in him from whom it is derived.

6. Love is rapid in its motion, as the bolt of heaven; it acts with ardour, alacrity, and freedom, and no created power is able to obstruct its course. It giveth all for all, and possesseth all in all: for

it possesseth the supreme good, from whom, as from its fountain, all good eternally proceeds. It respecteth no gifts, but, transcending all imparted excellence, turneth wholly to the giver of every perfect gift.

7. Love knoweth no limits, feeleth no burden, considereth no labour: it desireth to do more than, in its present state, it finds itself able to effect; yet it is never restrained by apparent impossibility, but conceiveth that all things are possible, and that all are lawful; it, therefore, attempteth every labour, however difficult, and accomplisheth many, under which the soul that loveth not, faints and falls prostrate.

8. Love is watchful, and though it slumbereth, doth not sleep: it is fatigued, but not exhausted; straitened, but not enslaved; alarmed by danger, but not confounded; and, like a vigorous and active flame, is ever bursting upwards, and securely passeth through all opposition.

9. He that loveth, feels the force of this exclamation, "My God! my love! Thou art wholly mine, and I am wholly thine!" and when this is the voice of love, it reacheth unto heaven.

DISCIPLE

10. Expand my heart with love, that I may feel its transforming power, and may even be dissolved in its holy fire! Let me be possessed by love, and ravished from myself by fervour and ecstasy! Let the lover's song be mine, "I will follow my beloved on high!" Let my soul rejoice exceedingly in love, and lose itself

in thy praise! Let me love thee more than myself; let me love myself only for thy sake; and in thee love all others, as that perfect law requireth, which is a ray of the infinite love that shines in thee!

CHRIST

11. Love delights in the communication of good; and, with a swiftness equal to thought, diffuses its blessings with impartiality and ardour. It is courageous and patient, faithful and prudent, long-suffering and generous, and never seeketh itself; for that which seeketh itself, falls immediately from love.

12. Love is circumspect, humble, and equitable; not soft and effeminate, fickle and vain, but sober, chaste, constant and persevering, peaceful and calm, and free from the influence of sensible objects. It is submissive and obedient to all, mean and contemptible in its own esteem, devout and thankful to God, resigned to God's will, and even when his consolations are suspended, faithfully dependant upon his mercy; for, in this fallen life, love is not exempt from pain.

13. He, therefore, that is not prepared to suffer all things, and, renouncing his own will, to adhere invariably to the will of his beloved, is unworthy of the name of lover. It is essential to that exalted character, to endure the severest labours and the bitterest afflictions, and to let nothing in created nature turn him aside from the supreme and infinite good.

5

Of the Trial of True Love

CHRIST

1. Thou art yet far distant, my son, from the fortitude and purity of love; for thou art always seeking after consolation with avidity; and the least opposition to thy inordinate desires, hath power to make thee relinquish thy most holy purposes. But he that hath the fortitude of love, stands firm in the midst of temptations; and utterly disbelieves and despises the flattering insinuations of the enemy: he knows that I love him; and whether in prosperity or adversity, makes me his supreme delight. And he that loves with purity, considers not the gift of the lover, but the love of the giver: he values the affection more than the tokens of it: esteems his beloved infinitely beyond the benefits he confers; and with a noble generosity, divesting his mind of all desires of personal advantage, reposes himself not upon my gifts, but upon me.*

---

* In the common Latin editions, and in all the English translations which I have seen, this, and the following chapter, are connected as one entire chapter upon "The trial of true love:" but M. Valart, the editor of the late Paris edition, has printed no more upon that subject than is here given; and has asserted, that one leaf, at least, is wanting in the old manuscripts, to make this chapter complete.—*Trans.*

That the Soul Must Not Despair under the Infirmities of Nature and the Suggestions of Evil Spirits

CHRIST

1. THOU must not, therefore, think that all is lost, when the fire of devotion ceases to blaze, and thy heart is not elevated with that sensible fervour which thou art always coveting: for the pleasing rapture thou sometimes feelest, is the immediate effect of present grace, to give thee a foretaste of the permanent joys of beatified spirits; upon which thou must not invariably depend, because it cometh and goeth according to the good pleasure of my will. Thy principal concern and business is to struggle against the incidental evil motions of fallen nature, and the evil suggestions of fallen spirits; and if thou dost this with faithful perseverance, thou wilt give true proof of that Christian fortitude which will be distinguished by the crown of victory.

2. Let not, therefore, strange phantasms, that possess thee against thy will, of whatever they are born, disturb the quiet of thy soul: maintain only a firm and unchangeable resolution of obedience, and an upright and pure intention towards God, and all will be well. Nor art thou to consider thyself as abandoned to the illusions of evil spirits, when, being suddenly elevated into holy ecstasy, thou as suddenly fallest into thy accustomed insensibility and dissipation: for this change thou rather sufferest than contributest to produce; and while it is involuntary, and thou strivest against it, instead of being a proof of the loss of grace, it may be made an occasion of humble and acceptable resignation.

3. Know, that it is the continual labour of thy inveterate enemy, to suppress every holy desire in thy soul, and divert thee from every holy exercise; from affectionate meditation on my sufferings, from the imitation of my life, and the persevering constancy of the saints, from the profitable recollection of thy numerous sins, from the watchful keeping of thy own heart, and from the heaven born resolution of "pressing towards the mark for the prize of thy high calling." He disturbs thy thoughts by innumerable, vain and sensual images, to create in thee disgust and abhorrence of the restraints of holiness, and to withdraw thee from prayer, and the instructions of the oracles of God: he is offended and alarmed at an humble and contrite acknowledgment of sin; and, if possible, would bring thee to a total disuse of the memorials of my death. Believe him not, nor heed his power, though, to ensnare thy soul, he thus continually spreadeth his deceitful net. When he suggesteth vain thoughts, and impure desires, charge all the guilt upon his own head, and say to him, "Get thee behind me, unclean and malignant spirit! And

be confounded at the foul whispers of thy unholy breath. Depart from me, most detestible seducer! Thou shalt have no part in me: for Jesus, the bruiser of thy head, is with me; and, like a mighty warrior, he will protect me from thy malevolence, and thou shalt fall subdued and confounded before him. I would rather die in extremity of torment, than consent to thy impious will. Hold thy peace, therefore, and be dumb for ever; for I will hearken to thee no longer, nor have any more converse with thee, though thou shouldst continually invent new stratagems to rob me of holiness and peace." "The Lord is my light and my salvation; of whom shall I be afraid? Though an host should encamp against me my heart shall not fear. The Lord is my strength and my Redeemer."

4. Thus, like a valiant soldier, let nothing abate thy struggle for victory; and if thou sometimes fallest through human frailty, rise immediately with redoubled vigour, depending upon the more abundant succours of my grace. Only beware of pride and self-complacence: for by these many are betrayed into error, till they are brought to a degree of blindness that is almost incurable. Let the destruction of the proud, vainly presuming upon their own wisdom and their own strength, be to thee a perpetual admonition of the blessings of humility.

7

Of Concealing the Grace of Devotion under the Veil of Humility

CHRIST

1. My son, when the fire of devotion is kindled in thy heart, let not the favour exalt thee into pride: boast not of it to others, as a distinction due to thy superior merit; nor ponder it in thy own mind with self-approbation and complacence; but rather conceal it; and in a true knowledge and distrust of thy great weakness, be more fearful in consequence of the gift, as bestowed upon one that may make an unworthy use of it. That ardour is not to be relied on, which may soon abate, and give place to coldness.

2. During the enjoyment of heavenly consolation, recollect how poor and miserable thou wert without it. But the advancement of the spiritual life dependeth not upon the enjoyment of consolation; but upon bearing the want of it, with such resignation, humility and patience, as not to relinquish prayer, or remit any

of thy accustomed holy exercises; thou must, therefore, with a willing mind, and the best exertion of thy ability, perform all thy duties; and not abandon the care of thy improvement, upon pretence of present barrenness and disquietude. There are many, who, when their state of grace does not correspond with their eager desires, and boundless expectations, instantly fall either into impatience or sloth: but "the way of man is not in himself:" and it belongeth unto God to give comfort when he pleaseth, to whom he pleaseth, and in that degree which is most subservient to the designs of his wisdom and goodness.

3. Some inconsiderate persons, by an improper use of the grace of devotion, have destroyed all its salutary effects: with an intemperate zeal grounded upon it, they have laid claim to such perfection as it is impossible to attain in the present life; not considering their own littleness, but following the tumultuous fire of animal passions, instead of the calm irradiations of divine truth. These, by presumption and arrogance, have lost the grace that was vouchsafed them; and though they had exalted themselves "as the eagles, and set their nest among the stars," yet they have fallen back into the poverty and wretchedness of nature; that being stript of all vain dependance upon themselves, they might learn, that the best efforts of human strength are ineffectual; and that none can soar to heaven, except I support his flight, and bear him upon my own wings.

4. They that are inexperienced in the spiritual life, will be soon deceived and easily subdued, unless they relinquish the guidance of their own opinions, and hearken to the counsels of tried and successful wisdom; but they who are "wise in their own con-

ceits," have seldom humility enough to submit to the direction of others. An understanding, therefore, that is able only to receive the truths of "the kingdom of God" with the meekness and simplicity of "a little child," is infinitely better than that which, arrogantly glorying in its extent, can comprehend the utmost circle of science: "better is it to be of an humble spirit" with the ignorant, "than to divide the spoils" of learning "with the proud."

5. That man acteth indiscreetly, who gives himself up to the joy of present riches, forgetful of his former poverty, and divested of that chaste and holy fear of God, which makes the heart tenderly apprehensive of losing the grace it has received. Nor has he attained the fortitude of true wisdom, who, in the day of distress and sadness, suffers his mind to be subdued by despair, and deprived of that absolute confidence in me, which is my right, and his own best support: but those that are most elate and secure in time of peace, are most fearful and dejected in time of war.

6. If thou wert always meek and lowly, and couldst keep thy spirit under the peaceful restraints of holy moderation, thou wouldst not so often incur danger, nor fall into sin. In the hour of spiritual fervour, it is useful to consider how it will be with thee, when those rays of comfort are withdrawn, and the shades of night succeed. And when that awful change takes place, thou must support thyself with the hope, that the light of day, which, for thy instruction and my glory, I have suffered to depart for a season, will break again upon thy soul with new effulgence.

7. The trial of this vicissitude of light and darkness, will contribute more to the perfection of thy spirit, than the gratification

of thy own selfish will in the enjoyment of perpetual sunshine; for the safety and blessedness of man's state in this life, are not be estimated by the number of his visions and consolations; nor by his critical knowledge of holy scripture, nor his exaltation to superior dignity and power; but by his being grounded and established in humility, and filled with divine charity; by seeking, in all he doth, the glory of God with purity and integrity; by his knowing and despising himself as nothing and vanity; and by his rejoicing more in contempt and abasement, than in honour and esteem.

DISCIPLE

8. "Shall I take upon me to speak unto my Lord, who am but dust and ashes?" If I deem more highly of myself, and arrogate any excellence; behold, thou standest in judgment against me, and my own iniquities oppose my claim by such a true and forcible testimony as I can neither contradict nor elude. But if I feel and acknowledge the darkness, impurity and wretchedness of my fallen nature; if I empty my heart of all self-esteem, and become humble as the dust of which I was made; then wilt thou look upon me with a favourable eye; then thy light will illuminate my heart; and then every degree of arrogance and self-esteem, however great, shall be swallowed up, and lost for ever, in the abyss of my own poverty. There thou showest me to myself, and teachest me what I am, what I have been, and from whence I came; for I am nothing, and knew it not.

9. When I am left to the disorderly workings of nature and self, behold, I am all weakness and misery! But when thy light breaketh upon my soul, my weakness is made strong, and my mis-

ery turned into joy. And transcendently wonderful it is, that a creature, which, by its alienation from thee, is always within the central attraction of selfishness and sin, should be so suddenly enlightened, purified and blessed, by a participation of the divine life! But this astonishing change is the pure effect of thy infinite love, preventing me in all holy desires, succouring me in all necessities, protecting me from imminent dangers, and delivering me from innumerable, unknown evils.

10. By the love of myself, I lost myself; but by the love and pursuit of thee alone, I have both found thee and found myself; and this love, the purer it hath been, the more truly hath it shown me my own nothingness; for thou, O most amiable Saviour, hast been merciful unto me, beyond all that I could either ask, hope, or conceive.

11. Blessed be thy name, O my God! that unworthy as I am of the least of all thy mercies, thou continuést to heap such innumerable benefits upon me. But thy love embraceth all, perpetually imparting life and blessings even to the ungrateful, and those that are wandered far from thee. O turn us back to thee again, that we may be thankful, humble, and wholly devoted to thy will, for thou art our wisdom, our strength, our righteousness, our sanctification and redemption.

8

That All Things Are to Be Referred to God, as the Ultimate End; and That the Service of God Is the Highest Honour, and the Most Perfect Freedom

CHRIST

1. IF thou wouldest be truly blest, my son, make me the supreme and ultimate end of all thy thoughts and desires, thy actions and pursuits. This will spiritualize and purify thy affections, which by an evil tendency are too often perverted to thyself and the creatures that surround thee; but if thou seekest thyself in the complacential honours of assumed excellence, or in the enjoyment of any good which thou supposest inherent in the creatures, thou wilt only find both in thyself and them the imbecility and barrenness of fallen nature. Refer, therefore, all things to me, as the giver of "every perfect gift;" the supreme good, from whom all excellence in the creatures is derived, and to whom alone the praise of excellence is due.

2. From me as from a living fountain the little and the great, the rich and the poor, draw the water of life; and he that willingly and freely drinks it to my glory, shall receive grace for grace; but he that glories in any thing distinct from me, or delights in any good not referred to me, but appropriated as his own, cannot be established in true peace, cannot find rest and enlargement of heart; but must meet with obstruction, disappointment and anguish, in every desire and every pursuit. Do not, therefore, arrogate any good to thyself, nor ascribe good to any other creature; but render all to me, thy God, without whom, not only man, but universal nature, is mere want and wretchedness. I, who have given all, demand it back in grateful acknowledgment, and require of every creature the tribute of humble thanksgiving and continual praise. In the splendour of this truth, all vainglory vanisheth, as darkness before the sun.

3. When divine light and love have taken possession of thy heart, it will no longer be the prey of envy, hatred and partial affections; for by divine light and love, the darkness and selfishness of fallen nature are totally subdued, and all its faculties restored to their original perfection. If, therefore, thou art truly wise, thou wilt hope only in me, and rejoice only in me, as thy everlasting life and light, perfection and glory; for "there is but one that is good, and that is God;" who is to be blessed and praised above all, and in all.

DISCIPLE

4. I will now speak again unto my Lord, and will not be silent; I will say to my king, and my God, who sitteth in the highest heaven, "O how great" and manifold are the treasures of "thy

goodness, which thou hast laid up for them that fear thee!" But what art thou, O Lord, to those that love thee with all their heart! Truly, the exquisite delight derived from that privilege of pure contemplation with which thou hast invested them, surpasseth the power of every creature to express.

5. How free, and how exalted above all blessing and praise, is that goodness which thou hast manifested toward thy poor servant; which not only called him into being, but, when he had wandered far from thee, by its redeeming virtue brought him back to thee again, and, with the command to love thee, conferred the power to fulfil it! O source of everlasting love! What shall I say concerning thee? How can I forget thee, who hast condescended to remember me, pining away and perishing in the poverty of sinful nature, and to restore me to the divine life I had lost! Beyond all hope thou hast shown mercy to thy servant, and beyond all thought hast made him capable of thy friendship, and dignified and blessed him with it. Poor and impotent as I am in myself, what can I render thee for such distinguishing grace? For it is not given unto all, to renounce this fallen state; and, in abstraction from the cares and pleasures of the world, to follow thee in "the narrow path that leadeth unto life."

6. But is it a foundation of boasting, thus to serve thee, whom all creatures are bound to serve? Instead, therefore, of considering this call from vanity and sin, with self-complacency and approbation, as a superior distinction from other men; I ought rather to be lost in admiration and praise of thy condescending goodness, which has received so poor and unworthy a creature

into thy family, and exalted him to the fellowship of thy faithful and beloved servants.

7. Lord, all that I have, all the ability by which I am made capable of serving thee, is thine; and thou, therefore, rather servest me. Behold, the heavens and the earth, which are continually ready to execute thy will, are made subservient to the redemption of fallen man; and, what is more, thy holy "angels are ordained ministering spirits, and sent forth to minister for them who shall be heirs of salvation!" and what infinitely transcendeth all, thou, the God of angels, hast condescended to take upon thee "the form of a servant" to man, and hast promised to give him thyself!

8. What returns of love and duty can I make thee, for these innumerable and astonishing dignities and blessings? O that I were able to serve thee all the days of my life; that I were able to serve thee truly, though but for one day! Thou art everlastingly worthy of all service, all honour, and all praise! Thou art my gracious Lord, and I am thy poor vassal, under infinite obligations to serve thee with all my strength, and perpetually to celebrate thy glorious name! To do this, is the sole wish and desire of my heart; and whatever ability is wanting in me to accomplish it, do thou in much mercy supply!

9. What exalted honour, what unsullied glory, to be devoted to thy service; and, for thy sake, to despise this fallen life, and all that is at enmity against thee? What large measures of grace are poured upon those, who voluntarily subject themselves to thy most holy laws! What ravishing consolations do they receive

from thy Holy Spirit, who, for the love of thee, renounce the delights of the flesh! What divine freedom do they enjoy, who, for the glory of thy holy name, leave "the broad way" of the world, "that leadeth to destruction," and entering in at "the straight gate," persevere in "the narrow way that leadeth unto life!"

10. O happy and honourable service, that makes man truly free and truly holy! O blessed privilege of filial adoption, that numbers him with the family of heaven, makes him equal to the angels, and renders him terrible to evil spirits, and delightful to all that are sanctified! O service for ever to be desired and embraced; in which alone we can recover the divine life we have lost, and enjoy the supreme and everlasting good!

9

That the Good Desires of the Heart Are to Be Carefully Examined and Regulated; and the Evil Subdued by Continual Resistance

CHRIST

1. SON, there are many things in which thou art not yet sufficiently instructed.

DISCIPLE

Lord, show me what they are, and enable me to understand and do them.

CHRIST

Thy desires must be wholly referred to me; and instead of loving thyself, and following thy own partial views, thou must love only my will, and in resignation and obedience be zealous to fulfil it.

2. When desire burns in thy heart, and urges thee on some pursuit, suspend its influence for a while, and consider, whether it is kindled by the love of my honour, or thy own personal advantage. If I am the pure principle that gives it birth, thou mayest yield thyself to its impulse without fear; and whatever I ordain, thou wilt enjoy the event in tranquillity and peace; but if it be self-seeking, hidden under the disguise of zeal for me, behold, this will produce obstruction, disappointment and distress. Beware, therefore, of trusting to the fervour of any new desire, before thou hast consulted me; lest thou disapprove and repent of that as evil, which thou hast eagerly admitted and ardently indulged as good; and as no desire must be immediately cherished, because it has the appearance of good, so neither must any, because it has not that appearance, be immediately suppressed. Even those desires and pursuits that are known to be good, it is often expedient to moderate and restrain; lest by too much impetuosity thou incur distraction, or by apparent irregularity give offence to others, or by unexpected opposition become impatient, and fall from thy holy purpose.

3. But it is always necessary to resist the sensual appetite, and by steady opposition subdue its power; to regard not what the flesh likes or dislikes, but to labour to bring it, whether with or against its will, under subjection to the spirit. And it must be thus opposed, and thus compelled to absolute obedience, till it is ready to obey in all things; and has learned to be content in every condition, to accept of the most ordinary accommodations, and not to murmur at the greatest inconvenience.

DISCIPLE

4. O Lord my God, from thy instructions, and my own experience, I learn the absolute necessity of patience; for this fallen state is full of adversity; and whatever care I take to secure peace, my present life is a continual trouble and warfare.

CHRIST

This, my son, will be the invariable condition of man, till every root of evil is taken from him. But peace, so far from being found in a state that is free from temptation, and undisturbed by adversity, is derived only from the exercise of much tribulation, and the trial of many sufferings. If thou sayest, thou art not able to suffer much here, how wilt thou be able to endure the purifying fire of an hereafter? Of two evils, the least is to be chosen; and to escape the awful punishments of futurity, thou must, for the sake of God, bear with equanimity and patience the evils of the present life.

5. Thinkest thou that the men of this world are exempt from suffering, or have but an inconsiderable portion? Thou wilt not find it thus, though thou searchest among the most prosperous and the most luxurious. But thou wilt say, that in the free indulgence of their own will, and the enjoyment of perpetual delight, their hearts are insensible to sorrow. And how long dost thou think, this uncontrolled licentiousness, and this uninterrupted enjoyment of sensual pleasure, will last? Behold, the mighty, the wise, and the rich, shall vanish like the cloud that is driven by the tempest, and there shall be no remembrance of their honours and delights! Even while they live, the enjoyment of what they have is embittered by the want of what they

have not; is either made tasteless by satiety, or disturbed by fear; and that from which they expected to derive pleasure and joy, becomes the source of pain and sorrow; for as this earthly and animal life is the fallen state of the human soul, it is just that the inordinate desire of its good should produce distraction and trouble; and that still wandering, and still unsatisfied, it should be its own torment.

6. O how transient and false, how impure and disgraceful are all these pleasures! And yet, wretched man, intoxicated by perpetual draughts, and blinded by custom, is insensible of the poison he imbibes; and for the momentary delights of an animal and corruptible life, incurs the danger of eternal death!

7. Do thou, therefore, my son, restrain the appetites of the flesh, and turn away from thy own will; "delight thyself in the Lord, and he shall give thee the desires of thy heart." If thou wouldst truly delight in me, and be plentifully enriched with the joys of my Spirit, know, that such blessedness depends upon the conquest of the world, and the renunciation of its sordid and transitory pleasures; and the more thou abandonest the desire of creaturely and finite good, the more truly wilt thou enjoy that infinite good which dwells in me.

8. But, to the enjoyment of infinite good, thou canst not attain at once; nor without much patient perseverance, and laborious conflict. Inveterate evil habits will produce an opposition, which can only be overcome by habits of holiness: the flesh will murmur and rebel; and it is only by increasing fervour of spirit that it can be silenced and subdued: the old serpent will deceive

and trouble thee, and tempt thee to revolt, but he must be put to flight by ardent prayer, and his future approaches must he opposed by continual vigilance, and continual employment in some holy exercise, or some innocent and useful labour.

10

Of Meek Obedience, after the Example of Jesus Christ; and of the Awful Consideration of the Divine Judgments, as a Motive to an Humble Opinion of Ourselves, and Our State in Grace

CHRIST

1. He that withdraws himself from obedience, withdraws himself from grace; and he that seeks his own fallen life, loseth that divine life which I came to restore. He that doth not freely and voluntarily submit to that superiority, under which my providence has placed him, demonstrates, that the flesh is not yet overcome, but frequently murmurs and rebels. If, therefore, my son, thou desirest to subdue thy own flesh, learn ready and cheerful submission to the will of thy superiors; for that out ward enemy will be much sooner overcome, if the mind is kept under strict discipline, and not suffered to waste its strength in dissipation

and indulgence. There is not a more violent or more dangerous enemy, than thy fleshly nature, when it does not freely consent to the law of the spirit: thou must, therefore, be established in true self-abasement, if thou wouldest prevail against flesh and blood.

2. It is the inordinate love thou still indulges for thy fallen self, that makes thee abhor submission to the will of others. But is it a great thing for thee, who art dust and ashes, to submit to man for the love of God, when I, the Supreme and Almighty, who created all things, submitted to man for the love of thee? I became the least and lowest of all, that human pride might be subdued by my humility. Learn, therefore, to obey, O dust! Learn to humble thyself, thou that art but earth and clay, and to bow down beneath the feet of all men! Learn to break the perverse inclinations of thy own will, that with ready compliance thou mayest yield to all demands of obedience, by whomsoever made. With holy indignation against thyself, suppress every intumescence of pride, till it can no longer rise up within thee; and thou art so submissive, so little and worthless in thine own eyes, that men may walk over thee, and as the dust of which thou art made, trample thee under foot. What hast thou to complain of, who art vanity itself? What, O base and unworthy sinner, canst thou answer to those who reproach and condemn thee, thou who has so often offended God, and incurred his terrible wrath? But thy life was precious in my sight, and my eye hath spared thee, that thou "mayest know my love, which passeth knowledge;" and in a perpetual sense of my mercy and thy own unworthiness, devote thyself to unfeigned humility and cheerful submission, and patiently bear the contempt of mankind.

3. Thou breakest the thunder of thy judgments over me, O Lord, and my bones are shaking with fear and trembling, and my soul is filled with unutterable dread. I stand astonished, when I consider, that the heavens are not clean in thy sight. If thou hast found folly and impurity in angels, and hast not spared even them, what will become of me? If the stars have "fallen from heaven," if "Lucifer, son of the morning," hath not kept his place; shall I, that am but dust, dare to presume upon my own stability? Many whose holiness had raised them to exalted honour, have been degraded by sin to the lowest infamy; and those that have fed upon the bread of angels, I have seen delighted with the husks of swine.

4. There is, therefore, no holiness, if thou, Lord, withdraw thy presence; no wisdom profiteth, if thy Spirit cease to direct; no strength availeth, without thy support; no chastity is safe, without thy protection; no watchfulness effectual, when thy holy vigilance is not our guard. For no sooner are we left to ourselves, than the waves of corruption rush upon us, and we sink and perish; but if thou reach forth thy omnipotent hand, we walk upon the sea and live. In our own nature we are unsettled as the sand upon the mountains, but in thee we have the stability of the throne of heaven: we are cold and insensible as darkness and death, but are kindled into light and life by the holy fire of thy love.

5. O how abjectly and meanly ought I to think of myself! How worthless and vain should I deem the good that appeareth to be mine! With what profound humility, O Lord, ought I to

cast myself into the abyss of thy judgments, where I continually find myself to be nothing, and am nothing! O depth immense! O fathomless and impassable gulf! In which my whole being is absorbed and lost. Where, now, is the lurking-place of human glory; where the confidence of human virtue? In the awful deep of thy judgments which cover me, all self-confidence and self-glory are swallowed up for ever!

6. Lord! what is all flesh in thy sight? Shall the clay glory against him that formed it? Can that heart be elated by the vain applause of men, that has felt the blessing of submission to the will of God? The whole world hath not power to exalt that, which Truth hath subjected to himself: nor can the united praise of every tongue move him, whose hope is established in thee: for those that utter praise, behold they also are nothing, like those that hear it! They shall both pass away and be lost, as the sound of their own words; but "the truth of the Lord endureth for ever."

11

That Our Desires Must Be Expressed in Terms of Absolute Resignation to the Divine Will

CHRIST

1. LET this, my son, be the language of all thy requests: "Lord, if it be pleasing to thee, may this be granted, or that withheld. Lord, if this tend to thy honour, let it be done in thy name. Lord if thou seest that this is expedient for me, and will promote my sanctification, then grant it me, and with it grace to use it to thy glory; but if thou knowest it will prove hurtful and not conduce to the health of my soul, remove far from me my desire." For every desire that appeareth to man to be right and good, is not born from heaven; and it is difficult always to determine truly, whether desire is prompted by the good Spirit of God, or the evil spirit of the enemy, or thy own selfish spirit; so that many have found themselves involved in evil, by the suggestions of Satan, or the impulse of self-love, who thought they were under the influence and conduct of the Spirit of God.

2. Whatever, therefore, presents itself to the mind as good, let it be desired and asked in the fear of God, and with profound humility; but especially, with a total resignation of thy own will, refer both the desire itself, and the accomplishment of it, to me, and say, "Lord, thou knowest what is best; let this or that be done, according to thy will. Give me what thou wilt, and in what measure, and at what time thou wilt. Do with me as thou knowest to be best, as most pleaseth thee, and will tend most to thy honour. Place me where thou wilt, and freely dispose of me in all things. Lo, I am in thy hands; do thou lead and turn me whithersoever thou pleasest: I am thy servant, prepared for all submission and obedience. I desire not to live to myself, but to thee: O grant it may be truly and worthily!"

DISCIPLE

3. Send me thy spirit, most merciful Jesus, "from the throne of thy glory," that it may be "present with me, and labour with me," and illuminate, sanctify, and bless me for ever! Enable me always to will and desire that which is most dear and acceptable to thee. Let thy will be wholly mine: let it reign so powerfully in me, that it may not be possible for me to oppose it, nor to like or dislike anything but what is pleasing or displeasing in thy sight!

4. Enable me to die to the riches and honours, the cares and pleasures of this fallen world; and in imitation of thee, and for thy sake, to love obscurity, and to bear contempt. But transcending all I can desire, grant that I may rest in thee, and in thy peace possess

my soul! Thou art its true peace, thou art its only rest; for, without thee, it is all darkness, disorder, and disquietude. In this peace, O Lord, even in thee, the supreme and everlasting good, I will "sleep and take my rest."

12

That True Comfort Is to Be Found Only in God

DISCIPLE

1. WHATEVER I can desire or conceive as essential to my peace, cannot be the production of this world, and in this world I seek not for it. If all the good of the present life was within my reach, and I had both liberty and capacity for its enjoyment, I know that it is not only changeable and evanescent, but is bounded by the grave. Thy full consolation, and perfect delight, therefore, O my soul, are to be found only in God, the comfort of the poor, and the exaltation of the humble. Wait a little while, wait, with patience and resignation, for the accomplishment of the divine promise, which cannot fail, and thou shalt enjoy the plenitude of good in heaven. By the pursuit of earthly and finite good, thou losest that which is celestial and infinite: use this, world, therefore, as "a pilgrim and a stranger," and make only the next the object of desire.

2. It is impossible thou shouldst be satisfied with temporal good, because thou wert not formed for the enjoyment of it: and though all that the creatures comprehend was in thy possession, thou wouldst still be unblest: for it is in the Creator, the supreme God alone, that all blessedness consists; not such as is extolled and sought after by the foolish lovers of the world, but such as the faithful Christian admires and sighs for; such as the spiritual and pure in heart, whose "conversation is in heaven," have sometimes a foretaste of.

3. How vain and transient is all human comfort! How substantial and permanent, that which is derived from the Spirit of Truth, living and ruling in the soul! The regenerate man continually turneth to Jesus, the Comforter within him, and saith, "Be present with me, Lord Jesus! in all places, and at all times. May I find consolation, in being willing to bear the want of all human comfort. And if thy consolation also be withdrawn, let thy will and righteous probation of me, be to me as the highest comfort, for 'thou will not always chide, neither wilt thou keep thine anger for ever!'"

CHRIST

4. Son, suffer me always to dispose of thee, according to my will; for that which is most profitable and expedient for thee, is known only to me. Thy thoughts are the thoughts of a man, and partial affections too often pervert thy judgment.

DISCIPLE

5. Lord, all thy words are truth! Thy care over me, is infinitely greater than all the care I can take for myself: and his

dependance is utterly vain, who casteth not all his care upon thee.

6. Bring my will, O Lord; into true and unalterable subjection to thine, and do with me what thou pleasest; for whatever is done by thee cannot but be good. If thou pourest thy light upon me, and turnest my night into day, blessed be thy name; and if thou leavest me in darkness, blessed also be thy name; if thou exaltest me with the consolations of thy Spirit, or humblest me under the afflictions of fallen nature, still may thy holy name be for ever blessed!

CHRIST

7. This absolute resignation, O my son, must be the prevailing temper of thy spirit, if thou wouldst live in union with me; thou must be as ready to suffer, as to rejoice; as willing to be poor and needy, as to be full and rich.

DISCIPLE

8. Lord, I will freely suffer, for thy sake, whatever affliction thou permittest to come upon me: I will indifferently receive from thee, sweet and bitter, joy and sorrow, good and evil; and for all that befalleth me, I will thank the love that prompts the gift, and reverence the hand that confers it. Keep me only from sin, and I will fear neither death nor hell; cast me not off for ever, nor blot my name out of the book of life, and no tribulation shall have power to hurt me.

13

That, in Conformity to the Example of Christ, the Miseries of This Fallen Life Are to Be Borne with Patience and Resignation

CHRIST

1. I CAME down from heaven, my son, for thy salvation, and took upon me the miseries of thy sinful nature, not from constraint but love, that thou mightest learn patience, and bear without murmuring the evils of thy fallen state. From the hour of my birth in the flesh, to the hour of my expiration on the cross, I found no intermission of sorrow; I felt the extreme want of the necessaries of life; I heard the continual murmurings of the world against me in silence, and bore with meekness its reproach and scorn; my benefits were treated with ingratitude, my miracles with blasphemy, and my heavenly doctrine with misrepresentation and reproof.

2. O Lord! since thou, in whom was no sin, hast, by a life of patience and obedience fulfilled thy Father's will: it is meet that I, a most wretched sinner, should patiently fulfil thy will, and bear the evils of my fallen state, till the purposes of thy redeeming love are accomplished.

3. Though the present life be in itself a grievous burthen, yet, through the power of thy grace, and the influence of thy holy example, and of the saints who have followed thy steps, it is made supportable and light even to the weak. It is also enriched with comforts that were not experienced under the law, when the gate of paradise remained shut, and the way to it was obscured with shadows, and so few desired to seek after the kingdom of God. Nor could even those whom thou hadst chosen to salvation, and numbered among the just, "enter into the holiest," till, by thy stupendous passion, and bitter death, "a new and living way was consecrated" for them.

4. O what thankfulness and praise are we bound to render thee, who hast thus condescended to open for every faithful soul a good and sure way to thy eternal kingdom? Thy life, O Lord! is our true way; and in the exercise of that holy patience which thy Spirit inspires, we approach nearer to thee, who art our righteousness and crown of glory. If thou hadst not shown us the path of life, and led us on by the united aid of thy example and thy grace, who could have found it, or who would have desired or been able to walk in it? If, blest as we are, not only with the splendour of thy miracles and precepts, but with the

irradiations of thy own Spirit, we are still cold and sluggish, and indisposed to follow thee; what should we be, if we were left in the darkness of fallen nature?

CHRIST

5. What hast thou said, my son? In the contemplation of my passion, and of the sufferings of those who have "followed me in the regeneration," suppress thy complaints: "thou hast not yet resisted unto blood." What are thy labours, compared with those of the saints, who have been so powerfully tempted, so grievously afflicted, so variously tried and exercised? In the re-membrance of theirs which were so heavy, thou shouldst forget thy own which are so light. That thou thinkest thy own suf-ferings not light, is owing to the impatience of self-love: but whether they are light or heavy, thou must endeavour to bear all with patient submission.

6. The more truly thou disposest thyself to suffer, the more wisely dost thou act, and the greater will be thy recompense: by fortitude and habitual suffering, the severest evils are disarmed of their sting. Say not, "I cannot brook this injury from such a man; and the injury itself is what I ought not to bear; for he has done me irreparable wrong, and reproached me for evil that never entered my thoughts. From any other person I could have borne it without emotion; and there are many things that it is fit I should suffer." These are foolish distinctions, founded only on the nature of the offence, and the relation of the person who commits it; but regard not the virtue of patience, nor by whom it will finally be crowned.

7. He is not patient, who will suffer but a certain degree of evil, and only from particular persons. The truly patient man considers not by whom his trials come, whether by his superior, his equal, or his inferior; whether by the good and holy, or by the impious and the wicked: but whatever be the adversity that befalls him, however often it is renewed, or by whomsoever it is administered, he receives all with thankfulness, as from the hand of God, and esteems it great gain: for there is no suffering, be it ever so small, that is patiently endured for the sake of God, which will not be honoured with his acceptance and blessing.

8. If, therefore, thou desirest to obtain victory, make ready for the battle. The crown of patience connot be received where there has been no suffering; and if thou refusest to suffer, thou refusest to be crowned; but if thou wishest to be crowned, thou must fight manfully, and suffer patiently; without labour, none can obtain rest; and without contending there can be no conquest.

DISCIPLE

9. O Lord! make that possible to me by grace, which I find impossible by nature. Thou knowest, that I can bear but little, and by the lightest adversity am soon overwhelmed. Grant that every tribulation and chastisement may become lovely and desirable to me, for thy name's sake! For patiently to suffer affliction for thee, will heal the disorders of my soul.

14

Of Personal Infirmity, and the Miseries of the Present Life

DISCIPLE

1. "I WILL confess my transgressions unto the Lord," and acknowledge my infirmity.—How small are the afflictions by which I am so often cast down, and plunged in sorrow! I resolve to act with fortitude, and, by the slightest evil, am confounded and distressed. From the most inconsiderable events, the most grievous temptations rise against me; and whilst I think myself established in security and peace, the smallest blast, if it be sudden, hath power to bear me down.

2. Behold, therefore, O Lord! my abject state, and pity the infirmity which thou knowest infinitely better than myself! Have mercy upon me, that I sink not, that the deep may not swallow me up for ever! So apt am I to fall, so weak and irresolute in the resistance of my passions, that I am continually driven back in the path of life, and covered with confusion in thy sight;

and though sin does not obtain the full consent of my will, yet the assaults of it are so frequent, and so violent, that I am even weary of living in perpetual conflict. My corruption and weakness are experimentally known; for the evil thoughts that rush upon me, take an easy possession of my heart; but are, with difficulty, driven out again.

3. O that thou, the most mighty God of Israel, the zealous lover of faithful souls, wouldst look down with compassion on the labours and sorrows of thy servant, and perfect and fulfil his desire of re-union with thee! Strengthen me with heavenly fortitude, lest the old man, this miserable flesh which is not yet brought under subjection to the Spirit, should prevail and triumph over me: against him I am bound to struggle as long as I breathe in this fallen life.

4. Alas! What is this life, which knows no intermission of distress and sorrow! Where snares are laid, and enemies rise, both behind and before, on the right hand and on the left! Where, while one tribulation is departing, another cometh on; and before the adversary is withdrawn from one severe conflict, he suddenly sounds a new alarm. And can a life like this, thus imbittered with distress, thus filled with corruption, and subject to such a variety of evils, be the object of desire? Can it even deserve the name of life, when it is continually teeming with plagues and pains that terminate in death? Yet it is still loved and desired; and many place their whole confidence in it, and seek their supreme happiness from it.

5. The world, indeed, is frequently reproached for its deceitfulness and vanity; but while carnal affections govern the heart,

it is not easily forsaken. It is both loved and hated by those, who have neither inclination nor power to leave it; "the lust of the flesh, the lust of the eye, and the pride of life," being the offspring of the world, love it as their parent; but as these bring forth pain and misery, they bring forth also in union with them, disgust and hatred of the world. But alas! While the soul is devoted to the delights of sin, the love of the world still prevails; and because she is a stranger to the joys of the Spirit, and hath neither tasted nor conceived the transcendent sweetness of communion with God, she still adheres to the world, and notwithstanding her manifold disappointments, still hopes to find pleasures hidden under thorns.

6. Those only, who live to God in the continual exercise of faith and love, of patience, humility, resignation, and obedience, obtain the conquest of the world; and enjoy those divine comforts that are promised to every soul that forsakes all to follow Christ; and those only truly discern, how grievously the lovers of the world are mistaken; and in how many various ways they are defrauded of happiness, and left destitute and wretched.

15 *

That the Soul Must Seek Her Repose Only in God

DISCIPLE

1. WITH all endowments of nature, and all gifts of grace, at all times, and in all places, whether in heaven or on earth, thy repose, O my soul, is to be found only in the supreme God, the everlasting rest and blessedness of the saints!

2. O most lovely, and most loving Jesus! Grant me the will and power, above all created being, to rest in thee: above all health and beauty, all glory and honour, all power and dignity, all knowledge and wisdom, all riches and all arts: above all promise and hope, all holy desires and actions, all gifts and graces which thou thyself canst bestow, all rapture and transport which the heart is able to receive: above angels and arch-angels, and all the

---

* M. Valart has printed this chapter as a continuation of the preceding; but if it is not a distinct chapter, it seems to be more naturally connected with the chapter that follows, and with that it stands united is all the editions prior to M. Valart's.

hosts of heaven; above all that is visible and invisible; and finally above everything, which thou, my God, art not!

3. For thou, O Lord God! art above all, in all perfection! Thou art most high, most powerful, most sufficient and most full! Thou art most sweet, and most abundantly comforting! Thou art most lovely, and most loving; most noble, and most glorious! In thee all good centers, from eternity to eternity! And, therefore, whatever thou bestowest on me, that is not thyself; whatever thou revealest or promisest, while I am not permitted truly to behold and enjoy thee, is insufficient to fill the boundless desires of my soul, which, stretching beyond all creatures, and even beyond all thy gifts, can only be satisfied in union with thy all perfect Spirit.

15

That God Always Heareth the Prayer of the Humble

DISCIPLE

1. DEAREST Jesus, most beloved spouse of my soul, supreme source of light and love, and sovereign Lord of universal nature! O that I had the wings of true liberty, that I might take my flight to thee, and be at rest! When will it be granted me, in silent and peaceful abstraction from all created being, to "taste and see how good" thou art, O Lord, my God! When shall I be wholly absorbed in thy fulness! When shall I lose, in the love of thee, all perception of myself; and have no sense of anything but thine!

2. Now I groan continually, and bear with pain the burthen of my wretchedness: for innumerable evils spring up in this vale of sin and sorrow, that darken, deceive, and distress my soul; so that I can have no free access to thee, nor enjoy that ineffable communion with thee, which is the privilege and perfection of

beatified spirits. O let my sighs move thee, and the multiplied desolation which I suffer in this fallen life!

3. Holy Jesus, ineffable splendour of eternal glory, sole comfort of the wandering soul! My heart is lifted up to thee, and without voice speaketh to thee in "groanings that cannot be uttered!" How long will my Lord delay his coming? O may he come to me, his forlorn creature, and turn my sorrow into joy! May he reach forth his omnipotent hand, and bid the winds that howl about me, be silent; and the sea that threatens to devour me, be calm! "Come, O Lord Jesus, come quickly!" In thy absence, no day nor hour is joyful: for thou art my only joy; and without thee my table is empty! I am a wretched prisoner in the darkness of this fallen world, bound with the chains of sin and misery, 'till thou revivest me with thy presence, restorest me to liberty, and liftest up the light of thy reconciled countenance upon me.

4. Let those that prefer to thee the gratification of some prevailing desire after the enjoyments of the world, seek that happiness which they can never find; I will pursue no good, present nor future, but thee alone, my God, my hope, and everlasting salvation! Nor will I cease from my importunity, till thou turnest back to me again, and I hear thy blessed voice speaking within me.

CHRIST

5. Behold, I am here! Behold, I am come to help thee, because thou hast called upon me "in sincerity and truth." Thy tears, and the desire of thy soul, thy humiliation and contrition, which I never despise, have inclined me and brought me to thee.

DISCIPLE

6. Lord, I have called upon thee in my distress, and I desire truly to enjoy thee, for I am prepared to renounce all things for thy sake. It is thou who hast given me both the will and the power to seek after thee: and for ever blessed be thy name, O Lord! who, in the multitude of thy tender mercies, hast shown this transcendent kindness to thy fallen creature.

7. What hath thy servant to say more in thy presence, but to beg, that he may humble himself exceedingly before thee, and be ever mindful of his own darkness, impurity, and malignity. There is none like unto thee in all the wonders of heaven and earth; and all that thou doest, is, like thyself, supremely good: thy judgments are true, and thy providence governeth the whole universe, that it may finally partake of thy perfection and blessedness! Praise and glory, therefore, be unto thee, O wisdom of the Father, for ever! "Bless the Lord, all his works, in all places of his dominions: bless the Lord, O my soul!"

16

Of the Thankful Remembrance
of the Manifold Mercies of God

DISCIPLE

1. Open my heart, O Lord, in thy law, and teach me to walk in thy commandments. Give me understanding to know thy will, and to remember, with faithful recollection and profound reverence, thy innumerable benefits, as well general as personal, that I may be always able worthily to praise thee, and give thee thanks.

2. I know, indeed, and confess, that of myself I am not able to render thee due thanks and praise for thy smallest benefits: for I am less than the least of all thy mercies; and when I attempt to contemplate thy excellent majesty, my spirit fails, unable to sustain the vast idea.

3. All the faculties of mind and body, all the endowments of nature, and all the advantages of grace, are the gifts of thy hand,

and proclaim the infinite love and munificence of the Giver, from whom all good eternally proceeds; and though one receiveth more, and another less, yet it is all thine, and without thee the least portion cannot be enjoyed.

4. He that hath received greater gifts, hath no reason to glory in his own merit, nor to exalt himself above others, nor to insult his poorer brother who hath received less: for he is the greatest and best, who ascribes least to himself, and is most devout and humble in the acknowledgment and praise of that infinite liberality from which every good and perfect gift proceeds; he only who esteems himself the vilest, and the most unworthy of receiving the least favours, is best qualified to discern and bless the bounty which confers the greatest.

5. But he that hath received more sparingly, ought not, therefore, to be troubled, nor to murmur at or envy the larger portion of his more wealthy brother! But rather, in humble resignation to thy will, O God, extol that universal goodness, which is so abundantly, so freely and voluntarily, and without respect of persons, dispensed to all. Thou art the inexhaustible fountain of good: and for all that flows from it, thou only art to be praised. Thou knowest what is fit to be given, and what to be withheld; and why one hath more, and another less, it is not in us, but in thee only to discern, who hast weighed the ability and state of all creatures in thy righteous balance.

6. Therefore, O Lord God, I esteem it a signal mercy, that I do not possess many of those qualities and endowments, which in the eyes of men appear glorious, and attract admiration and

applause: and he that truly considers his own personal poverty and meanness, so far from being disquieted, grieved, and dejected, should rather derive comfort from this right perception of his fallen state: for thou, O God, hast chosen the poor in spirit, the humble, the self-despised, and the despised of the world, for thy intimate friends, and the children of thy family. Of this, thy own apostles are eminent instances, whom thou hast appointed to "sit on twelve thrones, judging the twelve tribes of Israel;" yet these passed a life of indignity and opposition without complaint; and were so humble, so meek, so free from malignant passions and selfish views, that they even rejoiced to "suffer shame" and reproach "for thy name;" and with ardent affection embraced that poverty which the world despises, and with unshaken patience endured those afflictions which the world abhors.

7. Nothing, therefore, should give so much joy to the heart of him that truly loveth thee, and is truly sensible of thy undeserved mercies, as the perfect accomplishment of thy blessed will, not only in his temporal, but in his eternal state; in which he should feel so much complacency and acquiescence, as to be abased as willingly as others are exalted; to be as peaceful and contented in the lowest place, as others are in the highest; and as gladly to accept of a state of weakness and meanness, that is destitute both of ability and reputation, as others do of the most splendid honours, and the most extensive power. The accomplishment of thy will, and the glory of thy name, should transcend all other considerations, and produce more comfort and peace, than all the personal benefits which have been, or can possibly be conferred.

17

Of Four Steps That Lead to Liberty and Peace

CHRIST

1. I WILL now teach thee, my son, the way to liberty and peace.

DISCIPLE

Gracious Lord! do what thou hast condescended to offer. Such instruction I shall rejoice to hear, for such instruction I greatly need.

CHRIST

Constantly endeavour to do the will of another, rather than thy own:

Constantly prefer a state of want to a state of abundance:

Constantly choose the lowest place, and to be inferior to all: and Constantly desire and pray, that the will of God may be perfectly accomplished in thee and concerning thee.

Verily, I say unto thee, he that doeth this, enters into the region of rest and peace.

2. Lord! this short lesson teacheth great perfection; it is expressed in few words, but it is replete with truth and fruitfulness; and if I could faithfully observe it, trouble would not so easily rise up within me; for as often as I find myself disquieted and oppressed, I know I have wandered from the straight path which thou hast now pointed out. But do thou, O Lord, who canst do all things, and evermore lovest the improvement of the soul, increase the power of thy grace, that I may be enabled to fulfil thy word, and accomplish the salvation to which thou hast mercifully called me.

3. "O God, be not far from me: O my God, make haste for my help!" For a multitude of evil thoughts have risen up within me, and terrible fears afflicting my soul. How shall I pass them unhurt? How shall I break my way through them, and adhere to thee?

4. I will go before thee, and humble the lofty spirits that exercise dominion over thee: I will break the doors of thy dark prison, and reveal to thee the secrets of my law.

5. Do, O Lord! what thou hast graciously promised; lift up the light of thy countenance upon my soul, that every thought which is vain and evil may vanish before it. This is my strength

and comfort, to fly to thee in every tribulation, to confide in thy support, to call upon thee from the lowest depth of my heart, and patiently to wait for the superior consolations of thy Spirit.

6. Illuminate me, most merciful Jesus! with the splendour of thy presence, and cast out all darkness from the secret dwelling of my heart. Restrain my wandering thoughts that are carried out after evil, and repulse the temptations that so furiously assault my soul. Fight thou my battles; and with thy own omnipotent arm scatter all my enemies, those deceitful lusts, and malignant passions, that are continually at work to betray and destroy me; that in thy power I may obtain peace, and my purified soul, as a living temple consecrated to thee, may resound with songs of thankfulness and praise!—Rebuke the storms that rise up within me: say to the raging sea, "Be still;" and to the north-wind, "Blow thou not;" and a heavenly calm shall instantly succeed!

7. Send forth thy light and thy truth, that they may "move upon" this barren "earth:" I am "earth, without form and void;" deep covered with darkness, till thou sayest, "Let there be light." Pour forth thy treasures from the throne of grace; water my heart with the dew of heaven, that the barren soul may produce good fruit worthy to be offered up to thee. Raise my fallen soul, oppressed with the burden of sin; draw all my desire after thee, and give me such a perception of the permanent glories of heaven, that I may despise and forget the fleeting vanities of earth! O force me from myself! Snatch me away from the delusive enjoyment of the creatures, who are unable to appease my

restless desires. Unite me to thyself by the indissoluble bonds of love; for thou only canst satisfy the lover, to whom the whole universe, without thee, is "vanity and nothing."

18

Of Avoiding a Curious Inspection into the Conduct of Others

CHRIST

1. Son, indulge not vain curiosity, nor surrender thy spirit to the dominion of unprofitable cares: "what is this or that to thee? Follow thou me." What, indeed, to thee, are the words, the actions, and characters, of the idle and the busy, the ignorant and the vain? The burthen of thy own sins is as much as thou canst bear, and thou will not be required to answer for the sins of others; why then dost thou perplex thyself with their conduct? Behold, I understand the thoughts afar off, and nothing that is done under the sun can escape my notice. I search the personal secrets of every heart, and know what it thinks, what it desires, and to what its intention is principally directed. All inspection, therefore, and all judgment being referred to me, do thou study only to preserve thyself in true peace, and leave the restless to be as restless as they will; they cannot deceive Omniscience; and whatever evil they have done or said, it will fall upon their own heads.

2. Hunt not after that, fleeting shadow, a great name; covet not a numerous acquaintance, nor court the favour, and affection of particular persons; for these produce great distraction and darkness of heart. I would freely visit thee with instruction, and reveal my secrets to thee, if, in abstraction from useless cares, thou didst faithfully watch my coming, and keep the door of thy heart open to receive me. Be wise; "watch and pray;" and humble thyself continually under the sense of thy numerous imperfections and wants.

19

In What True Peace of Mind, and Spiritual Perfection Consist

CHRIST

1. SON, I once said to my disciples, "Peace I leave with you; my peace I give unto you; not as the world giveth, give I unto you." Peace is what all desire; but the things that belong to peace, few regard. My peace dwells not but with the humble and the meek, and it is found only in the exercise of much patience. If thou wilt hearken to me, and obey my voice, thou mayest enjoy a large portion of true peace.

DISCIPLE

Lord! what shall I do?

CHRIST

2. Keep a strict guard over all thy words and actions; and let the bent of thy mind be to please me only, and to desire and seek after no good but me; and if, with this, thou refrainest from

censuring the words and actions of other men, and dost not perplex thy spirit with business that is not committed to thy trust, thou wilt but seldom feel trouble, and never feel much.

3. Indeed, to be wholly exempt from trouble, and suffer no distress, either of mind or body, belongs not to thy present life, in which is much evil; but is the prerogative of that perfect state, where evil is not known. Think not, therefore, that thou hast found true peace, when thou happenest to feel no burthen of sin or sorrow; that all is well, when thou meetest with no adversary; and that perfection is then attained, when thy life regularly corresponds with thy own inclinations: neither exalt thyself in thy own esteem as the peculiar favourite of heaven, because thou hast felt the raptures of devotion, and tasted the ineffable sweetness of spiritual fervour: for by these marks the lover of perfection is not known; nor doth perfection itself, and man's progress toward it, consist in such exemptions and enjoyments.

DISCIPLE

In what then, O Lord?

CHRIST

4. In offering up himself, with his whole heart, to the will of God; never seeking his own will, either in small or great respects, either in time or in eternity; but with an equal mind weighing all events in the balance of the sanctuary, and receiving both prosperity and adversity with continual thanksgiving.

5. If thou wert so courageous, so patient and persevering, that when deprived of spiritual comfort, thou couldst prepare thy heart

for severer trials, not justifying thyself, and extolling thy own ho-liness, as that which ought to have exempted thee from such suf-ferings, but justifying me in all my appointments; then wouldst thou walk in the direct path to true peace, and mightest support thy spirit with the sure hope of seeing my face again in unutterable joy. The ground of this high attainment, is an absolute contempt and forgetfulness of self; and when that is established, know, that thou wilt enjoy peace in as full abundance, as it can possibly be enjoyed in this state of exile from thy native heaven!

DISCIPLE

6. Lord! it is the prerogative of a regenerate man, never to relax in his desire after his first state in thee; and in the midst of the innumerable cares and dangers that surround him, to pass on without solicitude, not from insensibility, but by a power of liberty peculiar to the mind, that is delivered from inordinate affection to the creatures.

7. I beseech thee, therefore, O my most merciful God! to pre-serve me from the cares of this fallen life, that my thoughts may not be darkened and perplexed; from the importunate wants and necessities of the body, that I may not be ensnared by the love of sensual pleasure; and from all the impediments of the regenerate life, that I may not be subdued, and utterly cast down by trouble and despair. I mean not from those things only, which the vain men of this vain world pursue with all the energy of desire; but from those awful miseries, which, as the consequence of the penal sentence of mortality, so encumber and depress the soul of thy servant, that she cannot enter into the liberty of the Spirit.

8. O my God! benignity and sweetness inexpressible! Turn into bitterness all carnal consolation, which is perpetually drawing my mind from the desire of eternity, and by the intuitive communication of delight from some good of this present life, alluring me more and more, and binding me faster to herself. Let not, O my God! let not flesh and blood subdue me; let not the world, and the transient glory of it, deceive me; let not the devil, and his subtle reasoning, supplant me. Give me courage to resist, patience to suffer, and constancy to persevere! Give me, instead of all worldly comfort, the divine unction of thy Holy Spirit; and for all carnal love, pour into my heart the love of thy blessed name!

9. Behold, the care of food and raiment, which it is difficult to separate from decoration, and the indulgence of the sensual appetite, is grievous and burthensome to a fervent spirit! Grant me grace, therefore, to use all things pertaining to the body with moderation; and not anxiously to desire the possession of them, nor bitterly lament the want. To cast all away, the law of nature does not permit; for nature must be sustained; but to desire superfluity, and that which ministers to delight more than to use, thy holy law forbids, lest the flesh should grow insolent, and rebel against the spirit. In all these difficult and dangerous paths, let thy wisdom and power govern and direct me, that I may not deviate to the right hand nor to the left!

20

That Self-Love Is the Chief Obstruction to the Attainment of the Supreme Good

CHRIST

1. My son, thou must give all for all, and make an absolute surrender of self-possession, and self-enjoyment. The love of self is more hurtful to the soul, than the united power of the world: for the creatures of the world have no dominion over thee, but in proportion to the affection and desire with which thou adherest to them for thy own sake; if thy love was pure and simple, and fixed only upon me, no creature would have power to enslave thee. Covet not that which thou art permitted to enjoy: retain not the possession of that which will obstruct thee in the pursuit of true good, and rob thee of inward liberty. How wonderful is it, that from the depth of thy heart thou dost not resign thyself, and all thou canst desire and possess, to my will!

2. Why dost thou pine away in useless sorrow? Why is thy strength consumed by superfluous cares? Establish thyself in ab-

solute resignation to my good pleasure, and thou canst suffer no evil. But if, for thy own appropriate good, and the gratification of thy own will, thou desirest change of enjoyment, and seekest change of place, thou wilt always be tormented with anxiety, and made more restless by disappointment; for in all earthly good thou wilt find a mixture of evil to imbitter its possession, and in every place meet with some adversary to oppose thy will.

3. It is not, therefore, the acquisition nor the increase of external good, that will help thee to repose and peace; but rather the contempt of it, and rooting the very desire of it out of thy heart; and this is true, not only of the luxury of wealth, but of the pomp of glory, and the enjoyment of empty honour and delusive praise, which suddenly pass away with the fleeting world where they are sought.

4. Neither can change of place avail, if there is wanting that fervent spirit devoted to me, which makes all places alike. Peace sought for abroad cannot be found; and it will never be found by the heart, that while it is destitute of me, wants the very foundation upon which alone peace can be established. Thou mayest change thy situation, but canst not mend it: the evils which thou hast fled from, will still be found, and more may soon arise; for thou hast taken with thee the fruitful root of every evil, thy own unsubdued, selfish will.

DISCIPLE

5 "Uphold me, O God! with thy free Spirit. Strengthen me with might in the inner man," that being emptied of all selfish solicitude, I may no longer be the slave of restless and torment-

ing desires; but, with holy indifference, may consider all earthly good, of whatever kind, as continually passing away, and my own fallen life as passing with it: for there is nothing permanent under the sun, where "all is vanity and vexation of spirit."

6. But what wisdom, O Lord! can consider this truly, but that which "was present with thee, when thou madest the world; and knew what was acceptable in thy sight?" O send me this wisdom "from the throne of thy glory," that I may learn to know and seek thee alone, and thus seeking, find thee; that I may love thee, and delight in thee, above all beings; and that I may understand all that thou hast made, as it is in itself; and regard its various forms only according to that order, in which thy infinite mind hath disposed them.

7. Grant that I may carefully shun flattery, and patiently bear contradiction; that neither disturbed by the rude breath of impotent rage, nor captivated by the softness of delusive praise, I may securely pass on in the path of life, which, by thy grace, I have begun to tread.

21

That the Perverse Judgments, and Cruel Censures of Men, Are Not to Be Regarded

CHRIST

1. BE not impatient, my son, when men think evil of thee, and speak that which thou art not willing to hear. Thy own opinion of thyself should be much lower than others can form, because thou art conscious of imperfections which they cannot know. If thy attention and care were confined to the life of the internal man, thou wouldst not feel the influence of fleeting words that dissolve in air. In times of ignorance and wickedness like this, it is most wise to hear reproach in silence, and in full conversion of thy heart to me not to regard the judgment of men.

2. Let not thy peace then depend upon the commendation or censure of ignorant and fallible creatures like thyself, for they can make no alteration in thy real character. True peace, and

true glory, are to be found only in me; and he that, seeking them in me, loves not the praise of men, nor fears their blame, shall enjoy peace in great abundance: for by such love, and such fear, nothing but disorder and disquietude are produced.

22

Of Submission to God in the Hour of Tribulation, and Confidence in Returning Grace

DISCIPLE

1. BLESSED be thy name, O Lord, for ever, who hast permitted this tribulation to come upon me! I am not able to fly from it; but it is necessary for me to fly to thee, that thou mayest support me under it, and make it instrumental to my good. I am in deep distress, and my heart faints and sinks under the burthen of its sorrows. Dearest Father, encompassed thus with danger, and oppressed with fear, what shall I say?—O save me from this hour!—But for this cause came I unto this hour, that after being perfectly humbled, thou mightest have the glory of my deliverance. "Be pleased, O Lord, to deliver me!" Poor and helpless as I am, what can I do, and whither shall I go, without thee? O fortify me under this new distress; be thou my strength and my support; and whatever be its weight, whatever its continuance, I will not fear.

2. And now, what doth thy Spirit enable me to say? Lord, "thy will be done!" This tribulation and anguish I must bear as my due: O that I may bear it with patience till the dark storm be over-past, and light and peace succeed! Yet thy omnipotent arm, my God, my mercy, as it hath often done before, can remove even this trial from me, or so graciously mitigate its severity, that I shall not utterly sink under it: the more difficult it seems to me, the more easy to thee is this change "of thy right hand," O Most High!

CHRIST

3. "I am the Lord, a strong hold in the day of trouble:" when, therefore, trouble rises up within thee, take sanctuary in me. The support of heavenly consolation comes slow, because thou art slow in the use of prayer; and, before thou turnest the desire and dependance of thy soul to me, hast recourse to every other comfort, and from the world and thyself seekest that relief which neither can bestow. But thy own experience will convince thee, that no profitable counsel, no effectual help, no lasting remedy is to be found, but in me. When, therefore, I have calmed the violence of the tempest, and restored thy fainting spirit, rise with new strength and confidence in the light of my mercy; for I the Lord declare, that I am always near, to redeem all fallen nature from its evil, and restore it to its first state, with superabundant communications of life, light, and love.

4. Dost thou think, that "there is any thing too hard for me?" or that I am like vain man, who promiseth and performeth not? Where, then, and what is thy faith! O believe and pre-

serve! Possess thy soul in patience, and comfort will follow in its proper season. Wait for me; and, if I come not, wait; for I will at length come, and heal thee. That which afflicts thee, is a trial for thy good; and that which terrifies thee is a false and groundless fear: and what other effect doth thy extreme anxiety about the events of to-morrow produce, than the accumulation of anguish upon anguish? Remember my words, "sufficient unto the day is the evil thereof." It is unprofitable and vain, to be dejected or elevated by the anticipation of that which may never come to pass. such disorders of imagination are, indeed, incident to fallen man: but it is an evidence of a mind that has yet recovered no strength, to be so easily led away by every suggestion of the enemy; who cares not, whether it be by realities or fictions, that he tempts and betrays thee: whether it is by the love of present good, or the fear of future evil, that he destroys thy soul.

5. "Let not," therefore, "thy heart be troubled," neither let it be afraid. "Believe in me," whose redeeming power has "overcome the world," and place all thy confidence in my mercy. I am often nearest thee, when thou thinkest me at the greatest distance; and when thou hast given up all as lost in darkness, the light of life and peace is ready to break upon thee. All is not lost when thy situation happens to be contrary to thy own partial judgment and selfish will. It is sinful in itself, and injurious to thy peace, to determine what will be thy future condition, by arguing from thy present perceptions, to inhere in trouble, whatever be its cause, as if it was thy state of existence; and to suffer thy spirit to be so overwhelmed by it, as if all hope of emerging from it was utterly taken away.

6. Think not thyself, therefore, condemned to total dereliction, when I permit tribulation to come upon thee for a season, or suspend the consolations which thou art always fondly desiring; for this is the narrow way to the kingdom of heaven: and it is more expedient for my servants to be exercised with many sufferings, than to enjoy that perpetual rest and delight which they would choose for themselves. I, who know the hidden thoughts of thy heart, and the depth of the evil that is in it, know that thy salvation depends upon thy being sometimes left in the full perception of thy own impotence and wretchedness; lest in the undisturbed prosperity of the spiritual life, thou shouldst exalt thyself for what is not thy own, and take complacence in a vain conceit of perfection, to which man of himself cannot attain.

7. The good I bestow, I can both take away, and restore again. When I have bestowed it, it is still mine; and when I resume it, I take not away that which is thine; for there is no good of which I am not the principle and centre. When, therefore, I visit thee with adversity, murmur not, neither let thy heart be troubled; for I can soon restore thee to light and peace, and change thy heaviness into joy; but in all my dispensations, acknowledge, that I the Lord am righteous, and greatly to be praised.

8. If thou wert wise, and didst behold thyself and thy fallen state, by that light with which I, who am the truth, enlighten thee; instead of grieving and murmuring at the adversities which befall thee, thou wouldst rejoice and give thanks: nay, thou wouldst "count it all joy," that I thus visit thee with affliction, and spare thee not. I once said to the disciples whom I chose to attend my

ministry upon earth, "As the Father hath loved me, so have I loved you:" and I sent them forth into the world, not to luxury, but to conflict: not to honour, but to contempt; not to amusement, but to labour; not to take repose, but to "bring forth much fruit with patience." My son, remember my words!

23

That the Creator Is to Be Found in Abstraction from the Creatures

DISCIPLE

1. O MY God, what a superior portion of grace do I still want, to be able continually to turn to thee without adherence to the creatures; who, while they retain the least possession of my heart, keep me at a tremendous distance from thee. He truly desired this liberty, who said, "O that I had wings like a dove, for then would I fly away and be at rest!" And what can be more at rest, than the heart that in singleness and simplicity regardeth only thee? What more free, than the soul that hath no earthly desires? To be able, therefore, in peaceful vacancy, and with all the energy of my mind, to contemplate thee, and know that thou infinitely transcendeth the most perfect of thy works, it is necessary that I should rise above all created beings, and utterly forsake myself; for while I am bound with the chains of earthly and selfish affections, I find it impossible to turn and adhere to thee.

2. Few, my son, attain to the blessed privilege of contemplating the infinite and unchangeable good, because few totally abandon that which is finite and continually perishing. For this, a high degree of grace is necessary, such as will raise the soul from its fallen life, and transport it above itself. And unless man, by this elevation of spirit, is delivered from all adherence to the creatures, and united to God; whatever be his knowledge, and whatever his virtue, they are of little value: he must remain in an infant state, grovelling upon earth, while he esteems anything great and good but one alone, the eternal and immutable God: for whatever is not God, is nothing, and should be held as "less than vanity and nothing." The difference, therefore, between the meek wisdom of an illuminated mind devoted to me, and the pompous wisdom of a critical and classical divine, is as incommensurate, as between the knowledge that "is from above, and cometh down from the Father of Light," and that which is laboriously acquired by the efforts of human understanding.

3. Many are solicitous to attain to contemplation as an exalted state, who take no care to practise that abstraction, which is necessary to qualify them for the enjoyment of it: for while they adhere to the objects of sense, to external services, and the signs of true wisdom instead of the substance, rejecting the mortification of self as of no value, they adhere to that which principally obstructs the progress to perfection.

4. Alas, Lord! I know not at what our purposes aim, nor by what spirit we are led, we who have assumed the profession and

character of spiritual men, that we exert so much labour, and feel so much solicitude, about that which is external and perishing, but scarce ever retire to the sacred solitude of the heart, to know what passes within us. Irresolute and impatient as we are, after a slight recollection, we rush into the world again, unacquainted with the nature and end of the actions which we pretended to examine: we heed not by what our affections are excited, nor in what they terminate; but like those of old, "when all flesh had corrupted his way," an universal deluge overwhelms us, and we are lost in folly, impurity, and darkness. Our inward principle, therefore, being corrupt, it cannot but be, that our actions, which, as the symptoms of the want of spiritual health, flow from it, must be corrupt also; for it is only out of a pure heart that the divine fruits of a pure life can be brought forth.

5. We busily inquire what such a man hath done, but not from what principle he did it: we ask whether this or that man be valiant, rich, beautiful, or ingenious; whether he be a profound scholar, an elegant writer, or a fine singer; but how poor in spirit he is, how patient, how meek, how holy and resigned, we disregard as questions of no importance. Nature looks at the outward man, but grace only at the inward: nature dependeth wholly upon itself, and always errs: grace trusts wholly in God, and is never deceived.

24

Of Self-Denial, and the Renunciation of Animal Desire

CHRIST

1. WITHOUT a total denial of self, my son, thou canst not attain the possession of perfect liberty. All self-lovers and self-seekers are bound in chains of adamant; full of desires, full of cares, restless wanderers in the narrow circle of sensual pleasures, perpetually seeking their own luxurious ease, and not the interests of their self-denying, crucified Saviour; but often pretending this, and erecting a fabric of hypocrisy that cannot stand; for all that is not of God, must perish.

But do thou, my son, keep invariably to this short, but perfect rule: "Abandon all, and thou shalt possess all: relinquish desire, and thou shalt find rest." Revolve this again and again in thy mind, and when thou hast transfused it into thy practise, thou wilt understand all things.

DISCIPLE

2. Lord! this is not the work of a single day, nor an exercise for children; for in this short precept is included the high attainments of "a perfect man" in thee.

CHRIST

Start not aside, my son, nor be depressed with fear, when thou hearest of the way of the perfect; but rather be excited to walk in it, and, at least, to aspire after it with all the energy of desire. O that self-love was so far subdued in thee, that with pure submission, thou couldst adhere to the intimations of my will, as well in the government of thy spirit, as in the disposals of my providence with respect to thy outward situation! Thou wouldest then be pleasing and acceptable in my sight, and thy life would pass on in peace and joy. But thou hast still much to abandon, which must be wholly surrendered up to me, before that rest which thou so earnestly seeketh can be found. "I counsel thee," therefore, "to buy of me gold tried in the fire, that thou mayest be rich;" heavenly wisdom, which trampleth the earth, and its enjoyments, under her feet. Renounce all earthly wisdom, and all complacency both in the world and in thyself.

3. I have told thee, that what is low and vile in human estimation, is to be purchased at the expense of what is exalted and precious; and most vile and contemptible among men, most unworthy of thought and remembrance, is heavenly wisdom; that wisdom which vaunteth not herself, nor seeketh the applause of men; and which many "honour with their lips," but in their hearts renounce; and yet it is "the pearl of great price;" which, while thus despised and rejected by men, must be hidden from them.

25

Of the Instability of the Heart, and of Directing the Intention to God Alone

CHRIST

1. TRUST not, my son, to the ardour of a present affection, for it will soon be past, and coldness will succeed. As long as thou livest in this fallen world; thou wilt, even against thy will, be subject to perpetual mutability; now joyful, and now sad; now peaceful, and now disturbed; at one time ardent in devotion, at another insensible; to-day diligent, to-morrow slothful; this hour serious, and the next trifling and vain. But he that hath true wisdom, and deep experience in the spiritual life, is raised above the fluctuation of this changeable state: he regards not what he feels in himself, nor whence the wind of instability blows; but studies only, that his mind may be directed to its supreme and final good. And thus, in all the various events of this changeable life, he remains unchanged and unmoved, by directing aright the eye of his intention, and fixing it solely upon me.

2. In most men, this eye of the intention soon waxeth dim; it is easily diverted by intervening objects of sensual good, and it is seldom free from some natural blemish of self-seeking; thus, those Jews, who went to Bethany, to the house of Martha and Mary, went, not only to see and hear Jesus, but to gaze upon Lazarus, whom he had just raised from the dead. The eye of the intention, therefore, must be continually purified, till it becomes perfectly single, and beyond all intermediate objects of pleasure and profit, looks solely unto me.

26

That the Soul Which Loves God, Enjoys Him in All Things, and above All; and in Him Findeth Peace

DISCIPLE

1. BEHOLD, thou art my God, and my all! What would I desire more? What higher happiness can I possibly enjoy? O sweet and transporting sounds! But to him only who loveth "not the world, neither the things that are in the world," but thee. My God, and my all! Enough to say, for him that understandeth; and often to say it, delightful to him that loveth.

2. When blest with thy presence, all that we are and have is sweet and desirable; but in thy absence, it becomes loathsome. Thou calmest the troubled heart, and givest true peace, and holy joy. Thou makest us to think well of all thy dispensations, and to praise thee in all. Without thee, the highest advantages cannot please long; for to make them truly grateful, thy grace

must be present, and they must be seasoned with the seasonings of thy own wisdom.

3. What bitterness becomes not sweet to him, that truly tasteth thee: and to him by whom thou art not relished, what sweetness will not be bitter? The wise of this world, and those that delight in the enjoyments of the flesh, are destitute of the wisdom that enjoyeth thee; for in the world is found only vanity, and in the flesh death. But they who, by the contempt of the world and the mortification of the flesh, truly follow thee, know, that they are wise in thy wisdom; and find themselves translated from vanity to truth, from the flesh to the Spirit. These alone enjoy God; and whatever is found good and delightful in the creature, they refer to the praise and glory of the Creator. Great, however, infinitely great is the difference between the enjoyment of the Creator, as he is in himself, and as he is discovered in imperfect creatures; of eternity, and of time; of uncreated light, and of light communicated.

4. O Eternal Light, infinitely surpassing all that thou illuminatest, let thy brightest beams descend upon my heart, and penetrate its inmost recesses! O purify, exhilarate, enlighten, and enliven my spirit, that with all its power it may adhere to thee in raptures of triumphant joy! O, when will the blessed and desirable moment come, in which thou wilt satisfy me with thy presence, and be in me, and to me all in all? For till this is granted me, my joy cannot be full.

5. Wretched creature that I am! I find the old man still living in me; he is not yet crucified, he is not yet perfectly dead. The

flesh still strongly lusteth against the Spirit, still kindles the rage of war, and suffers not "thy kingdom within me" to be at peace!

6. But do thou, O God! "who controllest the power of the sea, and stillest the raging of its waves," arise and help me! "scatter thou those that delight in war!" O break them to pieces with thy mighty power!—Show forth, I beseech thee, the wonders of thy greatness, and let thy right hand be glorified for there is no hope nor refuge for me, but in thee, O Lord, my God!

CHRIST

7. As long as thou livest in this world, my son, thou canst not live secure, but wilt always have need of "the whole armour of God." Thou art encompassed with enemies, who assault thee behind and before, on the right hand and on the left; and if thou dost not defend thyself on every side with the shield of patience, thou canst not long escape some dangerous wound: if thy heart is not fixed upon me, with a true and unalterable resolution of suffering all things for my sake, thou wilt never be able to sustain the fury of the conflict, nor obtain the palm of victory that distinguishes the saints in bliss. Thou must, therefore, with a lively faith, and a holy resolution of conquering all opposition, pass through the various dangers that surround thee; and "to him that" thus "overcometh, I will give to eat of the hidden manna," while for the slothful and unbelieving is reserved the portion of various misery.

8. If thou seekest rest in this life, how wilt thou attain to the everlasting rest of the life to come? Thou must prepare thy heart for the exercise of many and great troubles, not for the enjoyment of

continual rest: true rest is to be found, not on earth, but in heaven; not in the enjoyment of man, or any other creature, but of God. For the love of God, therefore, thou must cheerfully and patiently endure labour and sorrow, persecution, temptation and anxiety, poverty and want, pain and sickness, detraction, reproof, humiliation, confusion, correction and contempt. By these the virtues of "the new man in Christ Jesus" are exercised and strengthened; these form the ornaments of his celestial crown; and for his momentary labour I will give him eternal rest, and endless glory for transient shame.

9. Dost thou expect to enjoy the consolations of the Spirit, as long as thou pleasest? My saints expected it not, neither did they enjoy it, but with humble resignation endured painful labours, severe temptations, and protracted desertions, confiding not in themselves, but in me; for they knew, that "the sufferings of the present time were not worthy to be compared with the glory that should be revealed in them." And wouldst thou enter into the immediate possession of that, which these men, after so many tears, and such severe conflicts, scarcely attained? "O wait on the Lord; be of good courage; and he shall strengthen thy heart." Distrust me not, neither depart from me; but continually devote both soul and body to my service, and my glory. "Behold, I come quickly, and my reward is with me:" and till I come, my Spirit will be thy comforter in every tribulation.

27

Against the Fear of Man

CHRIST

1. My son, fix thy heart stedfastly upon the Lord; and while thy own conscience bears testimony to thy purity and innocence, fear not the judgment of man. It is good and blessed to suffer the censure of human tongues; nor will the suffering itself be grievous to the poor and humble in spirit, who confideth not in himself, but in God.

2. The opinions and reports of men are as various as their persons, and are, therefore, entitled to little credit. Besides, it is impossible to please all: and though Paul endeavoured to please all men in the Lord, and was "made all things to all;" yet, with him, it was "a very small thing to be judged of man's judgment." This faithful servant laboured continually to promote the edification and salvation of men; but their unjust judgments, and cruel censures, he was not able to restrain; he therefore

committed his cause to God, who knoweth all things; and sheltered himself against the false suggestions of the deceitful, and the more open reproaches of the licentious, under the guard of patience and humility: yet he sometimes found it expedient to support his character, that he might not give occasion of scandal to the weak, who are too apt from silence to infer guilt.

"Who, then, art thou, that thou shouldst be afraid of a man that shall die, and of the son of man that shall be made as grass, which to-day is, and to-morrow is cast into the oven?" Fear God, who is "a consuming fire," and thou wilt no longer tremble at the terrors of man. What hurt can man do thee, by his most malignant censures, or his most cruel actions? He injureth himself more than he can injure thee; and whoever he be, he shall not escape the righteous judgment of God. Set God, therefore, continually before thy eyes, and strive not with the injustice of man; and though at present, thou art overborne by its violence, and sufferest shame which thou hast not deserved; yet suppress thy resentment, and let not impatience obscure the lustre of thy crown. Look up to me in the highest heavens, who am able to deliver thee from all evil, and will render to every one according to his deeds.

28

Perfect Freedom Can Only Be Obtained by a Total Surrender of Self-Will

CHRIST

1. "He that loseth his life, shall find it." Forsake thyself, my son, and thou wilt find me. Renounce all self-seeking, all peculiarity of possession, and thou shalt enjoy the true riches. For the moment thou hast made such an absolute surrender of thyself, as to leave no ground for resumption, thou wilt be qualified to receive those abundant measures of grace which I am ever ready to bestow.

DISCIPLE

2. How often, Lord, must I perform this solemn act of resignation, and in what instances is self to be thus relinquished?

CHRIST

At all times, my son, as well this hour as the next; and in all interests, not only of thy temporary, but thy everlasting state: I admit no exceptions, but expect to find thee divested of all that can be called thy own. And till thou art stripped of self-will, with respect both to thy outward situation, and the state of thy spirit, it is impossible that thou canst be mine, and I thine. The sooner, therefore, thou makest this surrender of thyself, and the more sincere and pure it is, the more acceptable will it be to me, and the greater, consequently, thy own gain.

3. Many boast of this act of resignation, who perform it with secret reservations; they place not their whole confidence in God, but keep back some supports of self-dependance. With others it is at first sincere: but as soon as the storms of temptation beat upon them, they resume the gift they had made; and, turning back to themselves, find they are at a vast distance from the path of liberty and peace which they had begun to tread. These cannot possibly attain the freedom of a pure heart, nor enjoy the transporting intercourses of my friendship; for without a total resignation and daily sacrifice of self, the beatific union cannot be formed.

4. I have said to thee often, and now say to thee again, forsake thyself, resign thyself, and thou shalt enjoy the plenitude of heavenly peace. Give all for all; seek nothing for thyself, call for nothing back; adhere firmly and unchangeably to me, as the condition of possessing me; and thus thou wilt attain the freedom of a heaven-born spirit, and darkness shall overwhelm thee no more. Let it be thy continual thought, thy living desire, thy unceasing prayer, that, stripped of all self-possession and self-enjoyment, thou mayest, naked, follow thy naked master: die to thyself, and live eternally to me. Then the phantoms of vain

imagination shall disappear, the tumult of evil passions subside, and the torments of anxiety be felt no more; then immoderate fear and inordinate love, shall alike be driven from their dwelling in thy heart.

29

Of Self-Government in the Concerns of the Present Life, and of Having Recourse to God in All Its Difficulties and Dangers

CHRIST

1. ENDEAVOUR, my son, in every place, and in every external employment and action to be inwardly free, and master of thyself; that the business and events of life, instead of ruling over thy spirit, may be subject to it. Of all thy actions, thou must be, not the servant and slave, but the absolute lord and governor; a free and genuine Israelite, translated into the inheritance and liberty of the sons of God; who stand upon the interests of time, to contemplate the glories of eternity; who cast only a hasty glance on the transitory enjoyments of earth, and keep their eye fixed upon the permanent felicity of heaven; and who, instead of making temporal objects and interests an ultimate end, render them subservient to some purpose of piety

or charity, even as they were ordained by God, the sovereign mind, who formed the stupendous fabric, in which nothing disorderly was left.

2. If thus, in all events, thou sufferest not thyself to be governed by appearances, nor regardest what is heard and seen with a carnal purpose; but in every difficulty and danger enterest immediately into the tabernacle with Moses, to consult the Lord, thou shalt often receive an answer from the divine oracle, and return deeply instructed, both in things present, and things to come. And as Moses always retired to that holy place, for the determination of doubtful and disputed questions, and fled to prayer for aid, in times of danger and wickedness: so shouldst thou also enter the sacred temple of thy heart, and, on the same occasions, fervently implore the guidance and support of divine wisdom and strength. Thou hast read, that Joshua and the children of Israel, "because they asked not counsel at the mouth of the Lord," were betrayed into a league with the Gibeonites, being deluded by fictitious piety, and giving hasty credit to deceitful words.

30

Against Anxiety and Impetuosity
in the Concerns of the World

CHRIST

1. COMMIT thy cause invariably to me, my son, and I will give it a right issue in due season. Wait, patiently, the disposals of my providence, and thou shalt find "all things work together for thy good."

DISCIPLE

Lord, I would most willingly resign my state, present and future, to thy disposal; for my own restless solicitude, and feeble reasoning, serve only to perplex and torment me. O that I took no thought for the events of to-morrow, but could every moment unreservedly offer up all I am to thy good pleasure.

CHRIST

2. Man vehemently labours, my son, for the acquisition of that which he desires; but possession defeats enjoyment, and his de-

sire, which is restless and insatiable, is immediately turned to some new object. It is, therefore, of great importance, to suppress desire and forsake self, in the most inconsiderable gratifications.

3. Self-denial is the basis of spiritual perfection; and he that truly denies himself, is arrived at a state of great freedom and safety. The old enemy, however, whose nature is most repugnant to that which is most good, never remits his diligence; but night and day forms the most dangerous ambuscades, if peradventure, in some moment of false security, he may surprise and captivate the unwary soul. I have, therefore, cautioned thee, continually to "watch and pray, that thou enter not into temptation."

31

That in Man There Is No Good; and That, Therefore, He Has Nothing in Which to Glory

DISCIPLE

1. "Lord, what is man, that thou art mindful of him; and the son of man, that thou visitest him?" What, indeed, is he, and what hath he done, that thou shouldst bestow upon him thy Holy Spirit?

What cause have I to complain, O Lord! when thou withdrawest thy presence, and leavest me to myself; or what can I remonstrate, when my most importunate requests are not granted? This only I can truly think and say: "Lord, I can do nothing, and have nothing; there is no good dwelling in me that I can call my own, but I am poor and destitute in all respects, and always tending to nothing; and if I was not quickened and formed to life and light by thy Spirit, I should immediately become dark and insensible as death."

2. "Thou, O Lord, art always the same, and shalt endure for ever." Thou art always righteous and good; with righteousness and goodness governing the whole universe, and ordering all its concerns by the counsels of infinite wisdom. But I, who in myself am more inclined to evil than to good, never continue in holiness and peace; I am changeable as the events of time that pass over me, and am tossed upon every wave of affliction, and driven by every gust of passion. Yet, Lord, I shall find stability, when thou reachest forth thy helping hand; for thou canst so firmly strengthen and support me, that my heart shall no longer change with the various changes of this fallen life, but being wholly turned to thee, shall in thee find supreme and everlasting rest.

3. Wherefore, if I could but perfectly abandon all human consolation, either from a purer love and devotion to thee, or from the pressure of some severe distress, which, when all other dependance was found ineffectual, might compel me to seek after thee; then might I hope to receive more abundant measures of confirming grace, and to rejoice in new and inconceivable consolations of thy Holy Spirit.

4. But thanks be to thee, O Lord, from whom all good proceeds, whenever my state is better than I have reason to expect. I am an inconstant and feeble man, and vanity and nothing before thee. What have I then to glory in? And why do I desire to be esteemed and admired? Is it not for nothing? And that, surely, is most vain. Vain glory is not only the vainest of all vanities, but a direful evil, that draws away the soul from true

glory, and robs it of the grace of heaven: for while man labours to please himself, he labours to displease thee; while he sighs for the perishing laurels of the world, he loses the unfading crown of thy righteousness.

5. True glory, and holy joy, are to be found only in thee; and man should rejoice in thy name, not in the splendour of his own imaginary virtues; and delight in no creature, but for thy sake. Praised, therefore, be thy name, not mine; magnified be thy power, not my work! Yea, for ever blessed be thy holy name; but, to me, let no praise be given! Thou art my glory, and the joy of my heart! In thee will I glory, and in thee rejoice, all the day long; and "of myself I will not glory, but in mine infirmities!"

6. Let men "seek glory one of another;" I will seek that "glory which cometh only from thee," my God. For all human glory, all temporal honour, all worldly grandeur is vanity and folly; and vanishes like darkness before the splendour of thy eternal majesty! O my truth, my mercy, my God! O holy and blessed Trinity! Fountain of life, light, and love! To thee alone be praise, honour, power, and glory ascribed, through the endless ages of eternity!—Amen.

32

Of the Contempt of All Temporal Honour, and the Renunciation of All Human Comfort

CHRIST

1. Grieve not, my son, when others are honoured and exalted, and thou art despised and debased. Lift up thy heart to me in heaven, and thou wilt not be disturbed by the contempt of men on earth.

DISCIPLE

2. Lord, I am surrounded with darkness, and easily betrayed into a vain conceit of my own dignity and importance; but when I behold myself by thy light, I know, that no creature has done me wrong; and, therefore, surely I have no cause to complain of thee. On the contrary, because I have heinously and repeatedly sinned against thee, all creatures may justly treat me as an enemy, and make war against me. To me only shame and confusion of face are due; but to thee, praise, and honour,

and glory. And till I am perfectly willing to be despised and forsaken of all creatures, as that nothing which in myself I truly am; I know, that my restless spirit cannot possibly be established in peace, nor illuminated by truth, nor brought into union with thee.

CHRIST

3. Son, if thou sufferest even a conformity of sentiments and manners, and the reciprocations of friendship, to render thy peace dependant upon any human being, thou wilt always be unsettled and distressed: but if thou continually seekest after me, the ever living and abiding truth, as the supreme object of thy faith and love, the loss of a friend will be no affliction, whether it happens by falsehood or by death. The affections of friendship must spring from the love of me; and it is for my sake alone, that any person should be dear in the present life, as there is no goodness in man but what he receives immediately from me. Without me, therefore, friendship has neither worth nor stability; nor can there be any mutual ardours of pure and genuine love, but what I inspire.

4. As far as the distinct improvement and perfection of thy own spirit is concerned, thou shouldst be so mortified to all these personal affections and attachments, as to be able to live sequestered from human converse; for the soul draws near to God, only in proportion as it withdraws from all earthly comfort: with so much higher exaltation doth it ascend to him, as, with deeper conviction of its inherent darkness and impurity, it descends into itself, and becomes viler and more contemptible in its own sight. But he that challengeth and appropriateth any

good to himself, bars the entrance to the grace of God; for the Holy Spirit chooses, for the seat of his influence, a contrite and humble heart.

5. If thou wert brought to a true sense of thy own nothingness, and emptied of all selfish and earthly affections, I would, surely, "come unto thee" with the treasures of grace, "and make my abode with thee:" but while thou fondly gazest upon and pursuest the creature, thou turnest from the presence and sight of the Creator. Learn, therefore, for the love of the Creator, to subdue this earth-born love of the creature, and thou wilt be qualified to receive the light of eternal truth. It matters not how inconsiderable the object of pursuit is in itself; while it is vehemently loved, and continually regarded, it corrupts the soul, and keeps it at an infinite distance from its supreme good.

33

Of the Vanity of Human Learning

CHRIST

1. BE not captivated, my son, by the subtlety and elegance of human compositions; for "the kingdom of God is not in word, but in power." Attend only to the truths of my word, which enlighten the understanding, and inflame the heart; which excite compunction, and pour forth the balm of true consolation. But read my word, not for the reputation of critical skill, and controversial wisdom, but to learn how to mortify thy evil passions; a knowledge of infinitely more importance, than the solution of all the abstruse questions that have perplexed men's minds, and divided their opinions.

2. When, however, thou hast meekly and diligently read my word, still thou must have recourse to me as the only principle of divine truth. I am he that teacheth man knowledge, and giveth to the simple that light and understanding which no human instruction can communicate. He who listeneth only to my voice,

shall soon become wise, and be renewed in the spirit of truth. But, woe be to them, who, instead of turning to me to learn what is my will, devote their time and labour to the vain theories of human speculation! A day will come, when Christ, the teacher of teachers, the light and Lord of angels, shall appear, and at his omniscient tribunal hear the lessons which conscience has given to all; and then "shall Jerusalem be searched with candles, the hidden things of darkness shall be brought to light;" and the clamorous tongue of reasoning and disputing man shall be silent as the grave!

3. I am he, who exalteth the humble and simple mind and suddenly imparteth to it such a perception of eternal truth, as it could not acquire by a life of laborious study in the schools of men. I teach not, like men, with the clamour of uncertain words, or the confusion of opposite opinions; with vain learning, or the ostentation of learning yet more vain; or with the strife of formal disputation, in which victory is more contended for than truth; I teach, in still and soft whispers, to relinquish earth, and seek after heaven; to loathe carnal and temporal enjoyments, and sigh for spiritual and eternal; to shun honour, and to bear contempt; to place all hope and dependance upon me, to desire nothing besides me, and above all in heaven and on earth most ardently to love me.

4. By an intimate and supreme love of me, some, have been wonderfully filled with divine knowledge, and spoken truths beyond the comprehension of man; and thus, by forsaking themselves, they have found that light, to which the most subtle disquisitions of their own minds could not lead them.

5. To some, I speak only of common truths; to others, of those that are singular and exalted; I make myself known to some, under the more familiar appearance of human forms; and by a sudden and immediate communication of divine light, open the deepest mysteries to others. Though my written word speaks the same language to all, yet without me it does not impart the same instruction; I, as the internal principle of light to angels and men, am the only teacher of divine truth; I search the heart, and comprehend the most secret thoughts; I am the author and finisher of every good work; and, for the ornament and perfection of my mystical body, I bestow upon the members of it "a diversity of gifts, dividing to every man severally as I will."

34

Of Disengagedness from the Business of the World, and the Opinions of Men

CHRIST

1. IT is expedient for thee, my son, to be ignorant of many things, and to consider thyself as "crucified to the World, and the world to thee." Like one deaf, let what is said pass by thee unnoticed, that thou mayest keep thy thoughts fixed on "the things that belong unto thy peace." It is better to turn away from all that produces perplexity and disturbance, and to leave every one in the enjoyment of his own opinion, than to be held in subjection by contentious arguments. If thou wert truly "reconciled to God," and didst regard only his unerring judgment, thou wouldst easily bear the disgrace of yielding up the victory in the debates of men.

DISCIPLE

2. O Lord! into what depths of this earthly life must we be fallen, that the loss of what is called its good, should be lamented

in the bitterness of sorrow; and the acquisition of it pursued with ardent desire, and unremitted labour; while the injury that in both is done to the immortal spirit, is either not felt, or so soon and so much forgotten, as scarce ever to be recollected more. "About many things," that have neither worth nor duration, we are perpetually vigilant and busy; while the "one thing" supremely "needful," is neglected and passed by as of no importance. The whole man plunges into the stream of sensual life; and unless thou awaken in him a sense of danger, and suddenly stop his course, he is borne away with the torrent, and is lost.

35

Of Credulity in the Promises and Professions of Men

DISCIPLE

1. Do thou, O Lord, "give me help from trouble; for vain is the help of man!" How often have I failed of support, where I thought myself sure of it; and how often found it, where I had least reason to expect it! Vain and deceitful, therefore, is all trust in man; but the salvation of the righteous, O Lord, is in thee! Blessed, therefore, be thy holy name, O Lord, my God, in all things that befal us! We are weak and unstable creatures, easily deceived, and suddenly changed.

2. Where is the man that, by his own most prudent care, and watchful circumspection, is always able to avoid the mazes of error, and the disorders of sin! But he, O Lord, that puts his whole confidence in thee, and in singleness of heart seeks thee alone, will not easily be betrayed into either; and though he chance to fall into some unexpected trouble, and be ever so

deeply involved in it; yet thy merciful hand will soon deliver him from it, or thy powerful consolations support him in it; for thou wilt not utterly forsake him that putteth his whole trust in thee. A comforter that will continue faithful in all the distresses of his friend, is rarely to be found among the children of men; but thou, O Lord, thou art most faithful at all times, and in all events; and there is none like unto thee in heaven or earth. O how divinely wise must be that holy soul, who could say, "My heart is firmly established, for it is rooted in Christ." If this was my state, I should no longer tremble at the threats of wrath, nor be disturbed by the calumnies of envy.

3. Who can foresee future events? Who can guard against future evil? If those evils that are foreseen, often hurt us, we cannot but be grievously wounded by those that are unforeseen. But, wretched creature that I am, why did I not provide more wisely for the security of my peace? Why have I given such easy credit to men like myself, who are all destitute both of wisdom and power, though many think us and call us angels? Whom ought I to have believed? Whom, Lord! But thee, who art the Truth, that can neither deceive, nor be deceived? But "all men are liars;" so frail and inconstant, so prone to deceive in the use of words, that hasty credit is never to be given, even to those declarations that wear the appearance of truth.

4. How wisely hast thou warned us, O Lord, to "beware of men!" How justly said, that "a man's enemies are the men of his own house!" And how kindly commanded us to withhold belief, when it is said, "Lo, Christ is here;" or, "lo, he is there!" I have learned these truths, not only from thy word, but at the expense

of peace; and I pray, that they may more increase the caution, than manifest the folly of my future conduct.

5. With the most solemn injunctions of secrecy, one says to me, "Be wary, be faithful; and let what I tell thee be securely locked up in thy own breast;" and while I hold my peace, and believe the secret inviolate, this man, unable to keep the silence he had imposed, to the next person he meets betrays both himself and me, and goes his way to repeat the same folly. From such false and imprudent spirits, protect me, O Lord! that I may neither be deceived by their insincerity, nor imitate their practises. Give truth and faithfulness to my lips, and remove far from me a deceitful tongue; that I may not do that to another, which I am unwilling another should do to me.

6. How peaceful and blessed a state must that man enjoy, who takes no notice of the opinions and actions of others; who does not indiscriminately believe, nor wantonly report everything he hears; who, instead of unbosoming himself to all he meets, continually looks up to thee, the only searcher of the heart; and who is "not carried about with every wind of doctrine," but studies and desires only, that everything, both within and without him, may be directed and accomplished according to thy will!

7. It is of great importance, Lord, for the preservation and improvement of thy heavenly gift, to shun the notice of the world; and instead of cultivating attainments that attract admiration and applause, to aspire, with continual ardour, after inward purity, and a perfect elevation of the heart to thee. How often has the growth

of holiness been checked, by its being too hastily made known, and too highly commended! And how greatly hath it flourished, in that humble state of silence and obscurity, so desirable in the present life, which is one scene of temptation, one continual warfare!

36

Of Confidence in the Righteous Judgment of God, under the Various Accusations of Men

CHRIST

1. PLACE all thy hope, my son, in my mercy, and stand firm against the accusations of men; for what are words, but percussions of the air, that are of short continuance, and leave no impression? If thou art guilty, resolve to make the accusation an occasion of amendment; if thou art innocent, resolve to submit to it willingly, and bear it patiently, for my sake. It is, surely, a little matter for thee, who hast not yet endured the lasting pain of cruel stripes, sometimes to bear the light buffetting of transient words. And could so small an affliction make such a deep impression upon thy heart, if thou wert not still carnal, and didst not set too high a value upon the favour and applause of men? Thou art afraid of being despised; and, therefore, canst not bear reprehension, but labourest to conceal thy iniquities, or paliate them by mean excuses. But examine now the state

of thy heart, and thou must confess, that the world still liveth in thee, and that a vain desire of pleasing men, is the governing principle of all thy actions; for whilst thou refusest to be brought to shame, and be buffetted for thy faults, it is evident that thou art not yet truly humbled, not yet "crucified to the world, nor the world to thee."

2. Give ear to my word, and thou wilt not be moved by ten thousand opprobrious words of men. Consider, if everything was said against thee that the most extravagant malignity can suggest, what hurt can it possibly do thee, if thou only let it pass without resentment, regarding it no more than a mote that floats in the sunbeams? Could it even pluck from thy head a single hair? He that liveth not in my presence manifested in his heart, is easily disturbed by the lightest breath of human censure; but he that referreth his cause to me, without the least dependance on his own partial judgment, shall be free from the fear of man. I am the sole judge of man's actions, and the discerner of his most secret thoughts; I know the nature, the cause, and the effect of every injury; and make a just estimate of the wrong that is done by the injurious, and sustained by the sufferer. The word of reproach came forth from me; it was uttered by my permission, "that the thoughts of many hearts might be revealed;" for though the innocent and the guilty shall be judged in the face of the whole world at the last day, yet it is my will to try both beforehand, by a secret judgment unknown to all but myself.

3. The testimony of man is fallible, partial, and changeable; my judgment is true, righteous, and permanent as my own being. In its general comprehension it is hidden to all, and in particular

parts known only to a few; yet it never errs, nor can possibly err, though in the sight of fools it seemeth not right. To me, therefore, thou must refer thy cause in all human accusation, and not trust to the blind and partial determinations of thy own mind. The righteous will never be moved by whatever befals him, for he knows that it comes from the hand of God; whether, therefore, he is falsely accused, he will not be cast down; or whether he is justly defended, he will not triumph; for he considereth, that "I, the Lord, search the heart, and try the reins;" that I judge not, as man judgeth, by deceitful appearances; and that, therefore, what is highly esteemed by him, is often abomination in my sight.

DISCIPLE

4. O Lord God, the consciousness of innocence is not sufficient to sustain me under the pressure of false accusation: be thou, therefore, O most righteous and most merciful judge, the Omniscient and Almighty, who knowest all the darkness, impurity, and frailty of man, be thou my confidence and my strength!

5. Thou knowest what I know not; thou knowest my secret faults, and how justly I deserve continual reprehension and rebuke: I ought, therefore, whether I think I deserve it or not, to humble myself under every reproof of man, and bear it with meekness. O pardon me, as often as I have not done this; and mercifully bestow upon me the grace of more perfect submission!

6. It is, surely, much safer for me to depend for deliverance from all my evil, upon the free and boundless mercy manifested in thy

sacred humanity; than presuming upon particular instances of imperfect righteousness, to justify myself before men, when there is so much evil in me that escapes the notice of my own mind: and though in many instances my conscience condemns me not, yet am I not, therefore, justified; because, without the merciful "gifts of righteousness" which is in thee, no man living "can be justified in thy sight."

37

That All the Afflictions of the Present State Are to Be Patiently Endured for the Hope of Eternal Life

CHRIST

1. My son, neither let the labours which thou hast voluntarily undertaken for my sake, break thy spirit, nor the afflictions that come upon thee in the course of my providence, utterly cast thee down; but make my promise to be with thee, and bless thee, thy strength and comfort in every duty, and in all events. I am an abundant recompense, above all comprehension, and all hope. Thou shalt not long labour here, nor groan under the pressure of continual trouble. Wait patiently the accomplishment of my will, and thou shalt see a speedy end of all evil: the hour will quickly come, when labour and sorrow shall cease; for everything is inconsiderable and short, that passeth away in the current of time.

2. What thou hast to do, therefore, do with all thy strength. Labour faithfully in my vineyard; I myself will be thy reward. Write,
read, sing my praises, bewail thy own sins, keep silence, pray in
the spirit, and with patient resolution bear all afflictions: eternal
life is worthy not only of such watchful diligence, but of the severest conflicts.

3. On a certain day known only to the Lord, the reign of the Prince
of Peace will commence; when, instead of the vicissitudes of day
and night, joy and sorrow, that are now known, there shall be
uninterrupted light, infinite splendour, unchangeable peace, and
everlasting rest. Then thou wilt no longer say, "who shall deliver
me from the body of this death?" nor exclaim, "woe is me, that
my pilgrimage is prolonged!" for "death shall be swallowed up
in victory," and "the corruptible will have put on incorruption."
Then "all tears shall be wiped away from thy eyes," and all sorrow
taken from thy heart; and thou shalt enjoy perpetual delight in the
lovely society of angels, and the "spirits of the just made perfect."

4. O! was it possible for thee to behold the unfading brightness
of those crowns, which the blessed wear in heaven; and with
what triumphant glory they, whom the world once despised, and
thought unworthy even of life itself, are now invested; verily,
thou wouldst humble thyself to the dust, and rather choose to be
inferior to all men, than superior even to one: instead of sighing
for the perpetual enjoyment of the pleasures of this life, thou
wouldst rejoice in suffering all its afflictions for the sake of God;
and wouldst count it great gain, to be despised and rejected as
nothing among men.

5. If thou hadst a true sense of these astonishing glories, which are offered thee as the object of thy faith and hope, and didst suffer the thought and desire of them to enter into the depths of thy heart, couldst thou dare to utter one complaint of the evil of thy own state? Is any labour too painful to be undertaken, any affliction too severe to be sustained, for eternal life? Or is the gain or loss of the kingdom of God, an alternative of no importance? Lift up thy thoughts and thy desires, therefore, continually to heaven: Behold, all who have taken up the cross and followed me, "the captain of their salvation," in resisting and conquering the evil of this fallen state, now rejoice, are now comforted, now secure, now at rest; and shall abide with me for ever in the kingdom of my Father.

DISCIPLE

6. O most blessed mansions of the heavenly Jerusalem! O most effulgent day of eternity, which night obscureth not, but the Supreme Truth continually enlighteneth! A day of perennial peace and joy, incapable of change and intermission! O that all temporal nature was dissolved, and this day would dawn upon us! It shineth now in the full splendour of perpetual light, to the blessed; but to the poor pilgrims on earth, it appeareth only at a great distance, and "through a glass darkly." The redeemed sons of heaven triumph in the perception of the joys of this eternal day, while the banished sons of Eve lament the bitterness and irksomeness of the day of time. The days of this life are, indeed, short and evil, teeming with distress and anguish; in which man is defiled with many sins, agitated with many passions, disquieted with many fears, tortured with many cares, embarrassed with many refinements, deluded with many vanities, encompassed with many errors, worn

out with many labours, vexed with many temptations, enervated with pleasures, and tormented with want!

7. O when will these various evils be no more? When shall I be delivered from the miserable slavery of sin? When, O Lord, shall I think and speak of thee alone? When shall I perfectly rejoice in thee? When shall I regain my native liberty? O when will peace return, and be established; peace from the troubles of the world, and the disorders of sinful passions; and universal peace, incapable of interruption; that "peace which passeth all understanding?" When, O most merciful Jesus! When shall I stand in pure abstraction from all inferior good, to gaze upon thee, and contemplate the wonders of redeeming love? When wilt thou be to me all in all? O when shall I dwell with thee in that kingdom, which thou hast prepared for thy beloved before the foundations of the world? I am left a poor and banished man in the dominions of my enemy, where perpetual war rages, and every evil has its birth.

8. O soften the rigour of my banishment, assuage the violence of my sorrow, for my soul thirsteth after thee; and all that the world offers for my comfort, would but add more weight to the burthen that oppresses me. I long, O Lord, to enjoy thee truly, but am not able to lay hold of thee: I would fain rise to a constant adherence to heavenly objects, but the power of earthly objects operating upon my unmortified passions, depresses me and keeps me down: my mind labours to be superior to the good and evil of this animal life, but my body constrains it to be subject to them. And thus, "wretched man that I am," while the spirit is always tending to heaven, and

the flesh to earth, my heart is the seat of incessant war, and I am become a burthen to myself!

9. O what do I suffer, when raising my soul to thee; a crowd of carnal images suddenly rush upon me, and intercept my flight! "O my God, be not far from me! Put not away thy servant in anger. Cast forth thy lightning, and scatter" the illusions of the enemy; "shoot out thine arrows, and destroy" his power! Call in my wandering thoughts and desires, and unite them to thyself; efface the impressions of worldly objects; give me power to cast away immediately the imaginations of wickedness! O Eternal Truth, establish me in thyself, that no blast of vanity may have power to move me! O Immaculate Purity, enter the temple of my heart, and let all that is unholy be driven from thy presence!

10. In merciful compassion to my great infirmity, pardon me, O Lord, whenever, in prayer, my thoughts have been engaged by any object but thyself! I must confess that my distractions are great and frequent; and instead of being present where I stand or kneel, I am carried to various places, just as my roving thoughts have led me. Where my thoughts are, there I properly am; and my thoughts are chiefly with that which I most love: those objects too soon recur, which corrupt nature or sinful habit have made delightful. Upon this ground it is, that thou, O Truth, hast expressly declared, that "where the treasure is, there will the heart be also." And accordingly I find, in the various revolutions of my changeable heart, that when I love heaven, I take pleasure in meditating on heavenly enjoyments; when I love the world I think on its advantages with delight, and with sorrow

on its troubles; when I love the flesh, my imagination wanders through its various pleasures; when I love the Spirit, my faculties are with holy joy devoted to spiritual exercises; whatever I chiefly love, of that I delight chiefly to hear and speak; and I carry home with me the diversified images of it, even to my most secret retirement.

11. But blessed is the man who can calmly dismiss all creatures from the dwelling of his heart, that thou mayest take possession of it; who resolutely denies his fallen self, and with a fervent spirit, endeavours to exclude all earthly objects, and suppress all earthly affections, that, free from distraction, he may continually offer thee the sacrifice of pure prayer, and be made fit to mingle with the choirs of angels, and celebrate thy praise for ever!

38

Of the Desire of Eternal Life, and of the Great Blessedness That Is Promised to Those Who Resolutely Strive to Obtain It

CHRIST

1. MY son, when thou perceivest the heaven-born desire of eternal life to be breathed into thee, and longest to be dissolved, that free from the dark covering of the body, thou mayest, without obscurity, contemplate my unchangeable brightness; open thy heart wide, and with all the eagerness of hunger, receive this holy inspiration. But, without any mixture of complacence, and self-admiration, let all thy thanks and praise be faithfully rendered to the Sovereign Goodness, which so mercifully dealeth with thee, so condescendingly visiteth thee, so fervently exciteth thee, and so powerfully raiseth thee up, lest, by the propensity of thy own nature, thou shouldest be immovably fixed to the earth: for this new principle of life within thee, is not

the production of thy own reasoning and thy own efforts; but is the pure offspring of divine grace, the free gift of redeeming love, to lead thee on to holiness, to fill thee with humility, to sustain thee in all conflicts with sinful nature, and enable thee to adhere to me with all thy heart, and serve me with fervent duty, and the absolute surrender of thy own will.

2. The fire of devotion is often ardent, my son; but the flame ascends not without smoke; thus, the desires of many, while they burn for the enjoyment of heaven, are sullied with the dark vapours of carnal affection; and that which is so earnestly sought from God, is not sought wholly and purely for his honour: and such is thy desire, however restless and importunate; for that cannot be pure, which is mixed with self-interest. Make not, therefore, thy own delight and advantage, but my will and my honour, the ground and measure of all thy requests; for if thou judgest according to truth, thou wilt cheerfully submit to my appointment, and always prefer the accomplishment of my will to the gratification of thy own desires.

3. I know thy desire, and thy groaning is not hid from me. Thou wouldst this moment be admitted into the glorious liberty of the sons of God; thou longest for the immediate possession of the celestial mansions, and the unfading pleasures of the heavenly Canaan: but thy hour is not yet come: a far different time must first take place; a time of probation, labour and contest. Thou wishest now to be filled with the sovereign good; but thou art not yet capable of enjoing it. I am that Sovereign God; wait patiently for me, till the kingdom of God cometh.

4. Thou must still be proved upon earth, and exercised with various troubles. Some measures of consolation shall be imparted, to animate and sustain thee in thy conflicts; but the plenitude of peace and joy is reserved for the future world. "Be strong," therefore, "and of good courage," as well in doing as in suffering that which is repugnant to fallen nature; for thou must now "put on the new man," with new perceptions, will, and desires.

5. While this important change is making, thou wilt often be obliged to relinquish thy own will, and do that which thou dislikest, and forbear that which thou choosest: and wilt often find, that the designs of others will succeed, and thy own prove abortive; that what others say shall be listened to with eager attention, but what thou sayest shall either not be heard, or rejected with disdain; that others shall ask once and receive; thou shalt ask often, and not obtain; that the tongue of fame shall speak long and loud of the accomplishments of others, and be utterly silent of thine; and that others shall be advanced to stations of wealth and honour, while thou art passed by as unworthy of trust and incapable of service.

6. At such trials, nature will be greatly offended and grieved; and it will require a severe struggle to suppress resentment: yet much benefit will be derived from a meek and silent submission; for it is by such trials that the servant of the Lord proves his fidelity in denying himself, and subduing his corrupt appetites and passions. The difficulty of destroying self is greatest, when thou sufferest a course of events, and beholdest a scene of human transactions, wholly contrary to thy own will; especially, when that which thou art required to concur with or

execute, seems either ill-timed, or of small importance. As thou art placed in a state of subordination, thou darest not resist the ruling power, but thou findest it painful perpetually to follow the beck of another, and either relinquish thy own sentiments, or act contrary to them.

7. But consider, my son, the speedy end of all these trials, and the everlasting peace and blessedness that will succeed; they will then, so far from being occasions of disquietude and distress, furnish the most comfortable encouragements to persevering patience. In exchange for that small portion of corrupt and self-ish will, which thou hast freely forsaken in this world, thou shalt always have thy will in heaven: there, whatever thou willest, thou shalt find; and whatever thou desirest, thou shalt possess: there thou shalt enjoy all good, without the fear of losing any part; there thy will being always the same with mine, shall desire nothing private and personal, nothing out of me, nothing but what I myself desire: there thou shalt meet with no resistance, no accusation, no contradiction, no obstruction; but all good shall be present at once, to satisfy the largest wishes of thy heart; there, for transient shame patiently endured, I will give immortal honour; "the garment of praise for the spirit of heaviness:" and for the lowermost seat, an everlasting throne; there the fruits of obedience shall flourish, the labour of penitence rejoice, and the cheerfulness of humble subjection receive a crown of glory. Now, therefore, bow thyself willingly under the power of every human being; nor regard who it is that hath commanded this or that; but let it be thy only care, to take all in good part, and to execute with a willing mind whatever is enjoined or requested, whether by thy superior, thy inferior, or thy equal.

8. Let one man seek after this gratification, and another after that; let this man glory in one imaginary excellence, and that in another, and let their self-applause be seconded by the praises of a thousand tongues: but do thou, my son, glory only in my name, and rejoice only in the contempt of thyself, and the accomplishment of my will; let it be all thy wish, that, whether in life or death, God may be always glorified in thee!

38 *

Of the Resignation of a Desolate Spirit to the Will of God

DISCIPLE

1. O LORD God, holy Father, be thou blessed now and for ever! For whatever thou willest is done; and all that thou willest is good. Let thy servant rejoice, not in himself, nor in any other creature, but in thee; for thou only art the object of true joy: thou, O Lord, art my hope and exultation, my righteousness, and crown of glory! What good doth thy servant possess, which he hath not received from thee, as the free and unmerited gift of redeeming love? All is thine, whatever has been done for me, or given to me. "I am poor and afflicted from my youth up:" and sometimes my soul is sorrowful, even unto death; and sometimes is filled with consternation and terror, at the evils that threaten to overwhelm me.

---

* M. Valart has printed this chapter as a continuation of the preceding. *Translator.*

2. I long, indeed, O Lord, for the blessings of peace; I earnestly implore the peace of thy children, who are sustained by thee in the light of thy countenance. Shouldst thou bestow peace; shouldst thou pour forth the treasures of heavenly joy; the soul of thy servant shall be turned to harmony, and devoutly celebrate thy praise. But if thou still withholdest thy enlivening presence, as thou art often pleased to do, he cannot "run the way of thy commandments;" but must smite his bosom in the dust, because it is not with him as it was yesterday and the day before, "when thy lamp shone upon his head," and "under the shadow of thy wings" he was hidden and protected from evil.

3. O righteous Father, ever to be praised, the hour of thy servant's trial is at hand! O merciful Father, ever to be loved, it is meet that, in this hour, thy servant should suffer something for thy sake! O Father, infinitely wise, and ever to be adored, that hour is now come, which thou didst foreknow from all eternity, in which thy servant shall be oppressed and enfeebled in his outward man, that his inward man may live to thee for ever? And it is necessary he should be disgraced, humbled, and brought to nothing in the sight of men; should be broken with sufferings, and worn down with infirmities; that he may be qualified to rise again in the splendour of the new and everlasting day, and be glorified with thee in heaven! Holy Father, so thou hast willed, and so thou hast ordained; and that is come to pass which thou thyself didst appoint!

4. It is thy peculiar favour to him whom thou hast condescended to choose for thy friend, to let him suffer in this world in testimony of his fidelity and love; and be the affliction ever so great, and however often and by whatever hand it is administered, it

comes not but from the counsels of thy infinite wisdom, and it is under the direction of thy merciful providence; for without thee, nothing is done upon the face of the earth. "It is," therefore, "good for me, O Lord, that I should be afflicted; that I may learn thy statutes," and utterly cast from me all self-confidence and self-exultation. It is good for me that "shame should cover my face;" that in seeking comfort, I may have recourse, not to men but to thee; and that I may also learn to adore in silence thy unsearchable judgments, who afflictest the just together with the unjust, and both in righteousness and truth.

5. I give thee thanks, O Father of mercies! That thou hast not spared the evil that is in me; but hast humbled sinful nature by severe chastisements, inflicting pains, and accumulating sorrows, both from within and from without; and of all in heaven and on earth, there is none that can bring me comfort, but thou, O Lord my God, the sovereign physician of diseased souls; "who woundest and healest, who bringest down to the grave and raiseth up again!" Thy chastisement is upon me, and thy rod shall teach me wisdom.

6. Behold, dearest Father, I am in thy hands, and bow myself under the rod of thy correction! O smite my back, and bend my stubborn neck, till my untractable spirit shall learn ready compliance with thy righteous will! Make me thy holy and humble disciple, as thou hast often done others, that I may cheerfully obey every intimation of thy good pleasure! To thy merciful discipline I now commend all that I am, and bless thee that thou hast not reserved me for the awful chastisements of the future world. Thou knowest the whole extent of being, and all

its parts, and no thought or desire passeth in the heart of man that is hidden from thy sight. From all eternity, thou knowest the events of time; thou knowest what is most expedient for my advancement in holiness, and how effectually tribulation contributeth to wear away the rust of corruption. Do with me, therefore, O Lord, according to thy own will; only despise me not for my sinful life, which thou alone perfectly understandest, and thou alone canst effectually change.

7. Grant, O Lord, that, from this hour, I may know only that, which is worthy to be known; that I may love only that, which is truly lovely; that I may praise only that, which chiefly pleaseth thee; and that I may esteem what thou esteemest, and despise that which is contemptible in thy sight. Suffer me no longer to judge by the imperfect perception either of my own senses, or the senses of men ignorant like myself; but enable me to judge both of visible and invisible things, by the Spirit of Truth; and, above all, to know and to obey thy will; for those who form their judgment only upon what they hear and see, are often mistaken; and the lovers of the world also err and are deceived, through their continual adherence to the objects of sense. How great an instance of this fallibility of judgment, is the glory that is given and received among men! For none is made great by the voice of human praise. When men extol each other, the cheat imposes upon the cheat, the vain flatters the vain, the blind leads the blind, the weak supports the weak; and such commendation produces not honour, but shame: for, as it is said by that holy servant, St. Francis, "Such as every man is in thy sight, O Lord, such, and no greater, is he in himself."

That When We Find Ourselves Incapable of the Higher Exercises of Devotion, We Should, with Humility, Practise the Lower; and Account Ourselves Rather Worthy of Affliction than Comfort

CHRIST

1. IT is not possible for thee, my son, to continue in the uninterrupted enjoyment of spiritual fervour, nor always to stand upon the heights of pure contemplation; but, through the influence of that evil nature into which thou art fallen, thou must sometimes feel thy poverty and weakness, and, though with weariness and regret, be compelled to drag the burthen of thy corruptible life. As long as thou art united to an earthly body, thy days will often be full of heaviness, and thy heart of sorrow; and unable to escape from thy prison of flesh and blood, thou

must still feel the severity of its restraints, and groan under the power of those carnal appetites that interrupt the exercises of the Spirit, and of those dark passions that intercept thy views of heaven.

2. In such seasons of weakness and sorrow, it is necessary for thee to take refuge in external exercises, and seek relief from the diligent practise of common duties; with assured confidence expecting my return, and with meek patience bearing this state of banishment to darkness and desolation, till I visit thee again, and deliver thee from all thy distress: for I will then make thee forget thy past sufferings in the enjoyment of profound peace; I will so fully open to thy mind the divine truths contained in my written word, that with "an enlarged heart" thou shalt begin to "run the way of my commandments," and in the joyful antici-pation of the heavenly life, thou shalt feel and confess, that "the sufferings of the present time are not worthy to be compared with the glory which shall be revealed in thee."

DISCIPLE

3. Lord, I am unworthy, not only of the superior comforts, but of the least visitations of thy Spirit; and therefore, thou dealest righteously with me, whenever thou leavest me to the poverty and wretchedness of my fallen life. Though, from the anguish of my soul, "rivers of tears" were to "flow day and night;" still thou wouldst deal righteously with me, if thou still shouldst withdraw thy consolations; for I am worthy only of stripes and afflictions, because I have frequently and obstinately resisted thy will, and in many things have heinously offended. From a faith-ful retrospection on my past life, I cannot plead the least title to

thy smallest favours. But "thou, O Lord, who art a God full of compassion, and plenteous in mercy, and not willing that any" of thy creatures "should perish," to make known the riches of thy goodness in the vessels of mercy, notwithstanding the unworthiness of thy servant, hast often vouchsafed to comfort him beyond all human measure or conception; for thy consolations infinitely surpass the consolations of men.

4. What, indeed, am I, O Lord! and what have I done, that thou shouldst bestow upon me any consolations? So far from being able to recollect the least goodness proceeding from myself, I have been always prone to evil, and insensible and sluggish under the sanctifying influences of thy grace. Should I say otherwise, thou wouldst stand in judgment against me, and there is none that would be able to support my cause. My sins, are, indeed, so numerous and aggravated, that they have even exposed me to everlasting wrath; much more have they rendered me unworthy of the society of thy faithful servants, from whom I ought to be driven as an object of universal scorn and contempt. Painful as it is to pride, thus to plead my iniquities against myself, yet truth compels me to it, and I can only implore forgiveness from thy infinite mercy.

5. But oppressed with guilt, and filled with confusion as I am, what shall I say? I have no power to utter more than this—I have sinned, O Lord, "against thee only have I sinned. Have mercy upon me, according to thy loving kindness, and according to the multitude of thy tender mercies, blot out all my transgressions." Bear with me a little while, that I may truly bewail my corruption and misery, "before I go to the land of

darkness," that is covered with the shadow of death. And from a sinner, laden with such aggravated guilt, what other reparation dost thou desire for his transgressions, and what other is he capable of, but a heart broken with holy sorrow, and humbled to the dust?

6. In true contrition and humiliation, the hope of pardon hath its birth: there the troubled conscience is set at rest: the grace that was lost is found again; man is delivered from the wrath to come; and God and the penitent soul meet together with a holy kiss. The humble sorrow of a broken and a contrite heart is thy chosen sacrifice, O Lord! infinitely more fragrant than clouds of burning incense; it is the precious ointment, with which thou desirest to have thy holy feet anointed. A broken and a contrite heart thou never didst, nor ever wilt despise. That is the place of refuge from the wrath of the enemy; and there all impurity, both of the flesh and of the spirit, is cleansed and washed away.

40

That the Grace of God Dwells Not with Those That Love the World

CHRIST

1. SON, my grace, which is infinitely pure, like the fountain from whence it flows, cannot unite with the love of sensual pleasure, and the enjoyment of the world. If, therefore, thou desirest to receive this heavenly gift, thou must banish from thy heart every affection that obstructs its entrance.

2. Choose a place of undisturbed privacy for thy resort; delight in retirement and solitude; and, instead of wasting thy invaluable moments in the vain and unprofitable conversations of men, devote them to prayer and holy intercourse with God, which will increase compunction, and purify thy conscience. That thou mayest live to me in purity and peace, rate the whole world at nothing, and abstract thy thoughts and desires from its cares and pleasures; for thou canst not live to me, whilst thou seekest delight in the transitory enjoyments of time and

sense. Thou must wean thy heart from all human consolation and dependance, and be able to forsake even thy most intimate associates and dearest friends. This duty, and the ground of it, I have already taught thee by my apostle Peter, who earnestly beseeches my faithful followers, to consider themselves as what they truly are, "strangers and pilgrims" in the world: and, in that character, to abstain from the indulgence of earthly and carnal affections, "which war against the soul."

3. With what confidence and peace shall that man, in the hour of his dissolution, look on death, whom no personal affection or worldly interest binds down to the present life! But the sensual and sickly soul is not capable of such abstraction: nor can the natural man conceive the power of this heaven-born liberty of spirit. When, however, he feels the desire of this inestimable privilege kindled within him, he must labour to renounce all partial affections and interests, of whatever nature or degree; and, above all enemies, guard against himself. When self is once overcome, the conquest of every other evil will be easy. This is the true victory, this the glorious triumph of the new man! And he, whose sensual appetite is kept in continual subjection to his spirit, and his spirit in continual subjection to my will, he is this mighty conqueror of himself, and the lord of the whole world.

4. If, with holy ambition, thou desirest to ascend this height of perfection, thou must set out with a resolved will, and first lay the axe to the root, that the hidden life of self may be cut off, and all desire of personal gratification in the enjoyment of earthly good, be utterly extirpated. From self-love, as the corrupt stock, are derived the numerous branches of that evil; which forms the

trials of man in his struggles for redemption; and when this stock is plucked up by the roots, holiness and peace will be implanted in its room, and flourish for ever with unfading verdure. But how few labour at this extirpation! How few seek to obtain that divine life, which can only rise from the death of self! And thus men lie bound in the complicated chains of animal passions, unwilling, and, therefore, unable, to rise above the selfish enjoyments of flesh and blood. But he that desireth to "follow me in the regeneration," with an enlarged heart, must endeavour to suppress and kill the evil appetites and passions of his fallen nature; and not by a partial fondness, which hath its birth from self-love, adhere to any creature.

41

Of the Different Characters and Operations of Nature and Grace

CHRIST

1. My son, observe, with watchful attention, the motions of nature and grace: for though infinitely different, they are yet so subtle and intricate, as not always to be distinguished, but by an illuminated and sanctified spirit. Men invariably desire the possession of good; and some good is always pretended, as the constant motive of their words and actions; and, therefore, many are deluded by an appearance of good, when the reality is wholly wanting.

2. Nature is crafty: she allures, ensnares, and deceives, and continually designs her own gratification, as her ultimate end. But grace walks in simplicity and truth; "abstains from all appearance of evil;" pretends no fallacious views, but acteth from the pure love of God, in whom she rests as her supreme and final good.

3. Nature abhors the death of self; she will not be restrained, will not be conquered, will not be subordinate, but reluctantly obeys when obedience is unavoidable. Grace, on the contrary, is bent on self-mortification; she continually resists the sensual appetite; she seeks occasion of subjection; she longs to be subdued, and even uses not the liberty she possesses; she loves to be restrained by the rules of strict discipline; and so far from desiring the exercise of authority and dominion, it is her continual wish, that in body, soul, and spirit, she may live in perfect submission to the will of God; and, for the sake of God, is always disposed to humble herself under the power of every human being.

4. Nature is always labouring for her own interest; and, in her intercourse with others, considers only what advantages she can secure for herself: but grace is wholly inattentive to personal profit and convenience; and regards that most, which is most subservient to the common good.

5. Nature, as her chief distinction, is fond of receiving honour and applause; grace faithfully ascribes all honour and praise to God, as his unalienable right.

6. Nature dreads ignominy and contempt, and cannot bear them even in the cause of truth, but grace rejoices to suffer reproach for the name of Jesus.

7. Nature courts idleness and rest; grace shuns idleness as the nurse of sin, and embraces labour as the condition of life.

8. Nature delights in the splendour of dress; she hates and despises what is coarse and vulgar, and wearies imagination in the contrivance of ornament. But grace thinks not of decorating that body, which is the disgrace and punishment of man; and, therefore, spontaneously puts on the most plain and humble garments, nor refuses even those that are disagreeable to the flesh, ill-fashioned, and decayed.

9. Nature regards only the good and evil of this temporal world; she is elated with success, and depressed by disappointment; and the least breath of reproach kindleth the fire of her wrath. But grace adheres not to the enjoyments of time and sense: she is unmoved either by loss or gain, and unincensed by the bitterest invectives; and she lives only in the hope of eternal life.

10. Nature continually seeks after those treasures, which may not only be corrupted by moth and rust, and stolen by thieves, but which are, in themselves, perishing and evanescent. Grace lays up all her treasures in heaven, where nothing perisheth, nothing fadeth; and "where neither moth nor rust do corrupt, nor thieves break through and steal."

11. Nature is covetous, she grasps at peculiarity of possession, and greedily takes what she hates to give away. Grace is benevolent and bountiful to all; assumes no propriety; is contented with the necessary supports of life, and esteems it "more blessed to give than to receive."

12. Nature is strongly disposed to the enjoyment of the creatures, to the gratification of sensual desire, and to incessant wan-

dering from place to place in quest of new delight. Grace is continually drawn after God and goodness; she renounces the influence of the creatures, relinquishes the interests of the world, abhors the indulgences of the flesh, restrains the desire of wandering, and even for shame declines being seen in places of public resort.

13. Nature, in the depths of distress, seeks all her comfort from that which produces animal delight: grace has no comfort but in God; and leaving below this visible world, seeks all her rest in the enjoyment of the Sovereign Good.

14. Nature always acts upon principles of self-interest; she does nothing good for its own sake; but for every benefit she confers, expects either a present recompense, or such an establishment in the favour and approbation of men, as will secure a future return of some superior good; and besides that which she hopes to receive back in kind, she desires to have her services and gifts highly esteemed and applauded. Grace, for the highest offices of charity and bounty, expects no recompense from men, but continually looks up to God, as her exceeding great reward; she has no temporal interests to secure, for she desires no greater share of the possessions of time, than is necessary to sustain her in her progress to eternity.

15. Nature exults in the extensive interest of numerous relations and friends; glories in dignity of station, and splendour of descent; fawns upon the powerful; caresses the rich; and, with partial commendation, applauds those most, that are most like herself. But grace loves her enemies, and, therefore, counts

not the number of her friends; she values not the splendour of station, and the nobility of birth, but as they are dignified by superior virtue; she favours the poor, rather than the rich: compassionates the innocent, more than the powerful; rejoices with him that obeys the truth, not with the hypocrite; and continually exhorts even the good, not only to "covet earnestly the best gifts," but in "a more excellent way," by divine charity, to become like the Son of God.

16. Nature, when she feels her want and misery, quickly and bitterly complains; grace bears, with meekness and patience, all the poverty and wretchedness of this fallen state.

17. Nature refers all excellence to herself; argues and contends for her own wisdom, and her own goodness; but grace, conscious of her divine original, refers all the excellence she has, to God: she does not arrogantly presume upon her own wisdom, and her own goodness, for she ascribes neither goodness nor wisdom to herself; she contends not for a preference of her own opinion to the opinion of another, but in her searches after truth submits every thought and sentiment to the correction and guidance of infinite wisdom.

18. Nature is fond of deep researches, and with eager curiosity listens to that which is new and strange; she affects to be busy about the rectitude of public opinions, and pretends to demonstrate truth by sensible experiment; she desires to be known as the guardian of men's minds from the imposition of religious error; and pursues those inquiries most, that most attract admiration and applause. But grace does not follow the cry of novelty,

nor suffer herself to be captivated by subjects of curious and refined speculation; she knows, that the lust of vain wisdom is derived from the old stock of human corruption; and that all that is new in this sublunary world, is no more than the varied forms of its own vanity and misery: she, therefore, restrains the busy activity of the senses; suppresses the vain complacence, and shuns the vainer ostentation of human learning; conceals, under the veil of humility, the gifts and graces of the Holy Spirit; and, in every observation and discovery, seeks only the fruits of holiness, and the praise and honour of God. She desires not that herself, and her own wisdom and goodness, may be proclaimed and celebrated; but that God may be blessed and glorified in all his gifts, who with pure love bestoweth all that is possessed both by angels and men.

19. Such is the transcendency of grace to nature! She is the offspring of the light of heaven, the immediate gift of God, the peculiar distinction of the elect, and the pledge of eternal happiness; by whose power, the soul is raised from earth to heaven, and from carnal transformed to spiritual. The more, therefore, nature is suppressed and subdued, the more grace lives and triumphs; and by super-added communications of light and strength, "the inward man is, day by day," more and more renewed after the Image of God.

DISCIPLE

20. O Lord, my God, who didst create me after thy own divine image, from which I am now fallen; mercifully bestow upon me the grace which thou has represented as so necessary to my restoration, that my most depraved nature, which is always

tending to sin and to perdition, may be totally subdued! I feel in myself "a law of sin warring against the law of my mind, and bringing me into captivity" to sensual and malignant passions, which I cannot resist, till thy Holy Spirit kindles in my heart another fire.

21. I have need of the continual operation of his sanctifying power, to overcome all the workings of revolted nature, which is disposed to evil from its birth. It fell in Adam; and fallen, descended from him to all mankind, who have increased its obliquity by voluntary and habitual sin; so that nature, which came forth from thee pure and blessed, and in union with the light of heaven, is now spoken of, to express to impurity, darkness, and misery of man; for, left to its own motions, it is ever seeking itself, and tending to the enjoyments of that animal and earthly state into which it is fallen. The small portion of that divine breath which panteth after thee, is like a spark of fire buried under a heap of ashes. This is the new nature born of the seed of the Eternal Word, mercifully reserved in the human soul as the only principle of its redemption; which, though surrounded with darkness, and repressed by animal passions, has yet some real discernment of the essential and immutable difference between good and evil, truth and falsehood; but not having received the full eradiation of Divine Light, nor recovered the strength and purity of its affections, it is feeble in its purposes of duty, and unable to fulfil even that which it approveth.

22. From this ground it is, O my God! that "I delight in thy law after the inward man," convinced that "the commandment is holy, just, and good," condemning all evil, and warring against

the practise of it; "but with the flesh I serve the law of sin," and submit to the rigorous tyranny of sensual appetite, instead of the mild government of thy spirit: from this it is, that "to will is present with me; but how to perform that which is good, I find not:" from this it is that I form many purposes of holiness; but upon the trial of my strength to accomplish them, am driven back by the least difficulty; and from this, that though I know the path that leads to the summit of perfection, and clearly discern by what steps it is to be ascended; yet, laden and oppressed with the burthen of my corruption, I am unable to make any progress in it. How indispensably necessary, therefore, is thy grace, O Lord! by whose power alone evry good work must be begun, continued, and perfected! Without that power, I can do nothing that is acceptable to thee; but with it, I can do all things.

23. O grace essentially divine! Thou hast all merit within thyself, and givest to the endowments of nature all their value: for what is beauty or strength, or wit, or learning, or eloquence, in the sight of God, where grace does not dwell! The endowments of nature are common to the evil and the good; but the ornaments of grace are the peculiar marks of the elect, and all that are distinguished by them shall inherit eternal life. The chief ornament of grace is charity; without which, neither the gift of prophecy, nor the power of working miracles, nor the knowledge of the profoundest mysteries, are of any profit; not even faith, and hope, and that zeal which bestoweth all its possessions to feed the poor, and giveth the body to be burned, are acceptable to thee, O God, without charity.

Come, then, O meekness of the Lamb of God! Thou who

makest the poor in spirit rich in goodness, and the rich in goodness poor in spirit; O come descend into my soul, and fill it with the light and comfort of thy blessed presence, lest it faint and perish in the darkness and barrenness of its fallen state!

24. O God of all grace and consolation! That I may find grace in thy sight, is the sum of my requests; for thy grace is abundantly sufficient to supply all my wants, if I were even destitute of every thing that nature loves and covets to obtain. Though I am tempted and troubled on every side, "yea, though I walk through the valley of the shadow of death," yet, while thy grace is with me, "I will fear no evil." She is my strength, my counsel, and my defence; mightier than all enemies, and wiser than all the wise! She is the revealer of truth, the mistress of holy discipline, the sanctifier of the heart, the comforter of affliction, the banisher of fear and sorrow, the nurse of devotion, the parent of contrition; without whose quickening power, I should soon become an unfruitful and withered branch upon the tree of life, fit only to be cast away, or thrown into the fire. Grant, therefore, O most merciful Lord, that thy grace may abide with me continually; and produce in me an earnest desire and longing after the renovation of thy divine image, which is almost effaced by sin!

42

That We Must Deny Ourselves, Take Up the Cross of Christ, and Follow Him

CHRIST

1. THE more thou forsakest thyself, my son, the nearer wilt thou approach to me. To abandon the desire of earthly good, is the only way to obtain inward peace; and to abandon thy own will, is the only way to become united to God: I would have thee, therefore, without the least reluctance or murmur, make an unreserved sacrifice of thyself to my will. Follow me; "I am the way, the truth, and the life." Without the way which I have opened, thou canst not return to paradise; without the truth which I communicate, thou canst not know the way; and without the life which I quicken, thou canst not obey the truth. I am the way which thou must go, the truth thou must believe, and the life thou must desire and hope for: I am the invariable and perfect way; the supreme and infallible truth; the blessed, the uncreated, and endless life, If thou continuest in my way, "thou shalt know the truth, and

the truth shall make thee free," and fit thee for the possession of eternal life.

2. This I have already declared in the sacred records of my precepts; and have also told thee, that, "if thou wilt enter into life, thou must keep the commandments;" if thou wilt know the truth, thou must "continue in my word; if thou wilt be perfect, thou must sell all that thou hast;" if thou wilt be my disciple, thou must "deny thyself;" if thou wilt keep thyself for eternal life, thou must hate thy temporal life; if thou wouldst be exalted in heaven, thou must humble thyself on earth; and if thou wilt reign with me, thou must take up thy cross, and suffer with me; for the path of light and glory is found only by the servants of the cross, who "through much tribulation must enter the kingdom of God."

DISCIPLE

3. Lord Jesus! thy way is narrow and painful, and despised by the world: do thou, therefore, enable me to walk in it, and with meekness and patience to bear the contempt of the world: "for the disciple is not above his master, nor the servant above his lord." Let thy servant be continually exercised in the study and imitation of thy most holy life, in which all his perfection and blessedness is centered. Whatever else I hear, or read, or think of, gives me neither instruction nor delight.

CHRIST

4. Son, "if thou knowest these things, happy art thou if thou doest them." "He that hath my commandments, and keepeth them, he it is that loveth me; and I will love him, and will manifest myself

to him," and make him sit down with me in the kingdom of my Father.

DISCIPLE

5. Lord, I beseech thee, that this gracious promise may be accomplished in thy servant! I have received the cross from thee; and by the strength of that almighty hand which laid it upon me, I have borne it, and will bear it even unto death. The life which thou quickenest in thy disciples, is, indeed, a continual cross to the appetites and passions of fallen nature; but it is the light that must guide them back to paradise. This important journey is begun: O suffer me not to look back with a partial and selfish fondness for the good of this world, however specious; lest I incur the dreadful disqualification for "the inheritance of thy kingdom."

6. Come, my beloved brethren, let us take courage, and hand in hand pursue our journey in the path of life: Jesus will be with us! For Jesus' sake we have taken up the cross: and for Jesus' sake we will persist in bearing it: he, who is our captain and our guide, will be our strength and our support. Behold, our king, who will fight our battles, leads the way! Let us resolutely follow, undismayed by any terrors; and let us choose death, rather than stain the glory of which we are made partakers, by deserting the cross.

43

Against Extravagant Dejection, upon Being Sometimes Betrayed by Human Weakness

CHRIST

1. HUMILITY and patience, my son, under adversity, are more acceptable to me, than much joy and fervour, when all is prosperous without, and peaceful within.

2. Why art thou offended and grieved at every little injury from men; when, if it were much greater, it ought to be borne without emotion? As fast as such evils arise, let their influence be banished from thy mind; they are not new; thou hast met with many, and, if thy life be long, shalt meet with many more.

3. When adversity stands not in thy path, thou boastest of thy fortitude; and canst also give excellent counsel to others, whom thou expectest to derive strength from thy exhortations: but no sooner do the same evils that oppressed them turn upon thyself,

than thy fortitude forsakes thee, and thou art destitute both of counsel and strength. O let the frequent instances of the power which the lightest evils have over thee, keep thee continually mindful of thy great frailty. No evil, however, is permitted to befal thee, but what may be productive of a much greater good.

4. When thou meetest with injury from the violence or treachery of men, exert all thy resolution to drive the thoughts of it from thy heart: but if it toucheth thee too sensibly, to be soon buried in forgetfulness, let it neither depress nor vex thee; and if thou canst not bear it cheerfully, at least bear it patiently. If any censure that is uttered against thee be too severe and cruel to be heard in silence, suppress thy indignation before it bursteth into flames; and suffer no expression of impatience and resentment to escape thy lips, that may give occasion of scandal to the weak. The storm that is thus raised within thee will soon subside, and the wounds thy heart has received from the arrows of reproach, shall be healed by the influence of restoring grace. I live for ever; ready to help thee upon all occasions, and to bestow more abundant consolations upon thee, if thou puttest thy whole trust in my aid, and devoutly callest upon me for it.

5. Keep thy mind calm and patient, and girded for severer conflicts. But because thou art often strongly tempted, deeply troubled, and easily subdued, thou must not, therefore, think that all is lost: thou art man, not God; a spirit fallen into a corrupt animal body, not a pure angel: and how canst thou expect to continue in one unchangeable state of holiness, when this was not the privilege of Lucifer in heaven, nor of Adam in paradise, who stood not long in their original perfection? Give up thyself

wholly to my mercy: I am he, who comforteth all that mourn; and raiseth to a participation of divine strength, all that are truly sensible of their own weakness.

DISCIPLE

6. Thy words, O Lord, distil as dew, and are "sweeter" to my taste "than honey, or the honeycomb." What would become of me, in the midst of so much darkness, corruption, and misery, without thy Holy Spirit to illuminate, sanctify, and comfort me? I will regard not what nor how much I suffer, if I can but be made capable of enjoying thee, my supreme and only good! Be mindful of me, O most merciful God! Grant me a safe passage through this vale of sin and sorrow, and in the true path conduct me to thy heavenly kingdom! Amen.

44

Against the Vain and Presumptuous Inquiries of Reason into Subjects That Are Above the Comprehension of the Natural Man

CHRIST

1. FORBEAR to reason, my son, upon deep and mysterious subjects, especially the secret judgments of God. Ask not why this man is forsaken, and that distinguished by a profusion of grace; why one is so deeply humbled, and another so eminently exalted. These things surpass the limits of human understanding; nor can the deepest reasoning investigate the proceedings of the Most High. When, therefore, such questions are either suggested by the enemy, or proposed by the vain curiosity of men, answer, in the words of the royal prophet, "Righteous art thou, O Lord, and just are thy judgments! The judgments of the Lord are true, and righteous altogether." My judgments are to be feared, not

discussed; for they are incomprehensible to every understanding but my own.

2. Forbear also to inquire and dispute concerning the pre-eminence of the saints; who is the most holy, and who the greatest in the kingdom of heaven. These questions produce the strife of unprofitable debate, and nourish the presumption and vain-glory of which they are born: and while one in the pride of human wisdom, insolently contends for the superior excellence of this saint, and another for that, it is impossible, but that envy-ings and dissensions must rise among those who should "love as brethren;" but I am not a God of dissension, but of peace; and the interests of peace are promoted by meekness and humility, not by strife and self-exaltation.

3. That love, which, with such passionate ardour, preferreth and exalteth one saint above another, is not born of the Spirit, but is earthly and sensual. I am he, who formed all the saints, I gave them grace, I have exalted them to glory: I conferred the peculiar excellence which distinguishes each, "preventing him with the blessings of goodness:" I knew my beloved before the birth of time; and chose those out of the world, who had not chosen me; I called them by the free determination of sovereign goodness, drew them with the cords of love, and led them in safety through various temptations: I poured upon them the consolations of my Spirit, and crowned the patience which I enabled them to exercise; I own the last as well as the first, and embrace every one with inestimable love; I alone, who am al-ways to be blessed and praised, am to be "admired and glorified in all my saints." He, therefore, who despiseth the least of these

my servants, honoureth not the greatest; for "I have made both the small and great, and care for all alike;" but by despising one member of the kingdom of heaven, he not only dishonoureth the rest, but dishonoureth me: for all are united, by divine charity, into one body, of which I am the head: all will desire the same unchangeable good; and all love one another in the unity of his Spirit, who is all in all.

4. They are raised far above the influenc of unredeemed nature, which is ever tending to the love of self; and are passed into my love, in which they dwell with unutterable peace and joy. This love no power is able to alter or suppress; for it is the inextinguishable fire of their own life, "delivered from the bondage of darkness," and restored to its union with eternal truth. Let not, therefore, vain and sensual men, who have no conception of higher good than is found in the selfish enjoyments of their earthly life, presume any longer to dispute concerning the state of the saints, and their different degrees of perfection and glory; their decisions are governed by the heat of animal passions, not directed by the Spirit of Truth; and they give honour to one saint, and take it away from another, in conformity to their predominant humour, or in subserviency to their prevailing interest.

5. There are some, indeed, in whom these mistaken notions and partial attachments proceed from ignorance, without any mixture of interest or design; who having attained but an inferior degree of illumination, know not the power of divine love. They are determined in the preference both of angels and men, by natural instincts, and those personal singularities which are the foundation of private friendship; and the same distinctions of opinion and

affection, are made in the characters of the glorified inhabitants of heaven, as prevail among the inferior characters of imperfect men on earth. But these characters are totally incommensurate; a truth which the unenlightened know not, and which the enlightened only know by the teaching of the Spirit of Truth.

6. Beware then, my son, of being led by vain curiosity to "search the things that are above thy strength;" and let all thy faculties be employed in that only needful and important inquiry, how thou thyself mayest be found in the kingdom of heaven, though in the least and lowest place. If it was possible for any one to know, who is the most holy, and who is the greatest there, what would that knowledge avail him, unless it made him more humble, and excited in him greater ardour to glorify my name? He, who, in constant attention to the state of his own soul, laments the multitude and enormity of his sins, and the small number and imperfections of his virtues; and when he thinks on the saints, thinks only how exceedingly remote he is from the perfection which they have attained; is more acceptable to me, than he who employs his time and thoughts in considering and disputing about the different degrees of excellence and glory, that distinguish the particular members of that illustrious assembly. It is infinitely more useful, and more safe, with tears and prayers to implore grace to imitate the great examples they have left upon earth; than to labour, by fruitless inquiries into their state in heaven, to know what no human understanding is able to comprehend.

7. The saints are highly blessed and perfectly content: and men should be content with the imperfect knowledge of their fallen

state, and suppress their vain curiosity, and refrain from their vainer disputes. They glory not in any personal excellence; for they arrogate no good themselves, but ascribe all to me, who with infinite liberality have freely given them whatever they possess: and the consummation of their own honour and happiness, is found in their boundless love of God, and their joyful celebration of his praise. The more exalted their state is, the more humble is their spirit, and the more conformable and dear to me; and therefore, it is written, that, "the four and twenty elders," who were seated round the throne of heaven, "cast their crowns before the throne, and fell down before him that sat on the throne, and worshipped him that liveth for ever and ever."

8. Many solicitously inquire, who is the greatest in the kingdom of heaven, that utterly neglect the only important inquiry, whether they themselves shall be thought worthy to be numbered among the least. To be the least, where all are great, is to be great; and all in heaven are great, for they are the adopted sons and heirs of God; "a little one shall become a thousand, and the child shall die an hundred years old; but the sinner an hundred years old shall be accursed."

9. When the disciples, whom I had chosen to attend my ministry upon earth, clamorously inquired, who should be "the greatest in the kingdom of heaven," it was answered, "Except ye be converted, and become as little children, ye shall not enter into the kingdom of heaven. But whosoever shall humble himself as a little child, the same is greatest in the kingdom of heaven." Woe be to them, therefore, who, in the pride of human attainments, disdain the spontaneous and meek humil-

ity of little children; for the gate of the kingdom of heaven is too low to give them entrance? "Woe unto them that are rich, who say they are increased in" mental "riches, and have need of nothing, for they have received their consolation;" and whilst the poor enter into the kingdom, they shall stand weeping and wailing without! But rejoice, ye humble, and leap for joy, ye poor in spirit! for while ye continue in the truth that has made you what ye are, "yours is the kingdom of God!"

45

That All Hope and Confidence Is to Be Placed in God Alone

DISCIPLE

1. LORD! what is my confidence in this life, and what my comfort in the possession and enjoyment of all things under heaven? Is it not thee alone, O Lord my God! whose mercies are without number, and without measure? Where hath it been well with me, when thou wert absent? Or where could it be ill, when thou wert present? I had rather be naked, hungry and despised with thee, than abound in honour, wealth and pleasure, without thee: would rather choose, with thee, to wander upon the earth, and have no place "where to lay my head," than, without thee, to possess a throne in heaven. But, where thou art, there is heaven; and death and hell are only there where thou art not. Thou art the desire of my soul; and to thee, my sighs and groans, my cries and prayers, shall continually ascend! There is none that is able to deliver me from my necessities; none in whose power and goodness I can trust, but thee, O my God!

Thou art my refuge and my hope in every distress; my most powerful comforter, and most faithful friend!

2. Men seek themselves, and their own interest; thou seekest only my redemption from the bondage of evil, and orderest all thy dispensations for its accomplishment. Though thou permittest me to be exposed to the trial of various troubles, yet thou mercifully superintendest the conflict, and directest the event for my supreme and everlasting good: "for whom thou lovest thou chastenest, and scourgest every son whom thou receivest." And in this awful probation, thou art not less to be loved and praised, than when thou fillest my soul with heavenly consolations. Thou alone, therefore, O Lord my God! art my hope and sanctuary: with thee I leave all my tribulation and anguish, and resign the beginning, continuance, and end of every trouble, to thy blessed will.

3. Wherever I look for support and consolation out of thee, I find nothing but weakness and distress: and if thou dost not revive, strengthen, illuminate, deliver and preserve me, the friendship of mankind can give no consolation; the strength of the mighty, bring no support; the counsels of the wise, and the labours of the learned, impart no instruction; the treasures of the earth, purchase no deliverance; and the most remote and secret places, afford no protection. All persons and things, that seem to promise peace and happiness, are in themselves vanity and nothing, and subvert the hope that is built upon them; but thou art the supreme, the essential, and final good; the perfection of life, light, and love! And the most powerful support of thy servants, is found in an unreserved and absolute dependance upon thee!

4. "Unto thee, therefore, do I lift up mine eyes, O thou that dwellest in the heavens!" In thee, my God, the Father of mercies, I place all my confidence! O illuminate and sanctify my soul, with the influence of thy Holy Spirit, that being delivered from all that darkness and impurity of its alienated life, which thy eyes cannot look upon, it may become the living temple of thy holy presence, the seat of thy eternal glory! In the immensity of thy goodness, O Lord! and "in the multitude of thy tender mercies, turn unto me," and hear the prayer of thy poor servant, who has wandered far from thee, into the region of the shadow of death. O protect and keep my soul amidst the innumerable evils which this corruptible life is always bringing forth; and by the perpetual guidance of thy grace, lead me in the narrow path of holiness, to the realms of everlasting light, love, and peace. Amen.

THE END.

About Thomas à Kempis

THOMAS À KEMPIS was born in the year 1380, at Kempis, or Kempen, a small walled town in the duchy of Cleves, and diocese of Cologne. His family name was Hamerlein, which signifies, in the German language, "a little hammer." His parents were named John and Gertrude Hamerlein. At thirteen years of age he began his studies, and about nineteen betook himself to a monastery of Augustine monks. About five-and-twenty he took the habit of that house and order. He continued there for the space of seventy years, particularly eminent for his piety, humility, diligent study of the Holy Scriptures, austerity of life, moving eloquence in discourse, and extraordinary zeal in prayer. His person was of a middle stature, of a strong brown complexion, and a lively piercing eye. His eyesight was so good, and he retained it so perfect to the last, that he never was reduced to the use of spectacles. He died August 8, 1471, in the ninety-second year of his age.

He was a canon regular of Augustines, and sub-prior of Mount St. Agnes' Monastery. He lived chiefly in the monastery of Mount St. Agnes; where his effigy, together with a prospect of the monastery, were engraven on a plate of copper that lies over his body. The said monastery is now called Bergh-Clooster; or, as we might say in English, Hill-Cloyster; many strangers in their travels visit it.

In the engraving on copper, above-mentioned, and lying over his grave, is represented a person respectfully presenting to him a label, on which is written a verse to this effect:

"*O! where is Peace! for thou its paths hast trod.*"

To which Kempis returns another label, inscribed as follows:

"*In poverty, retirement, and with God.*"

Kempis was certainly one of the best and greatest men since the primitive ages. His book "Of the Imitation of Christ," has seen near forty editions in the original Latin, and above sixty translations have been made from it into modern languages. He composed this Treatise in the sixty-first year of his age, as appears from a note of his own writing in the library of his convent.